THE WHAT TO EAT
IF YOU HAVE HEART DISEASE

COOKBOOK

THE WHAT TO EAT
IF YOU HAVE HEART DISEASE
COOKBOOK

Simple, Balanced, Heart-Smart Recipes and Meal Plans

DANIELLA CHACE, M.S.

CB
CONTEMPORARY BOOKS

Library of Congress Cataloging-in-Publication Data
Chace, Daniella.
    The what to eat if you have heart disease cookbook / Daniella
Chace.
        p.   cm.
    Includes index.
    ISBN 0-8092-9709-4
      1. Heart—Diseases—Diet therapy—Recipes.   I. Title.
RC684.D5 C48   2000
641.5'6311—dc21   00-31478
                                                   CIP

Cover design by John Gagné
Cover photograph copyright © Beth Galton Photography/Workbook CO/OP Stock

Published by Contemporary Books
A division of NTC/Contemporary Publishing Group, Inc.
4255 West Touhy Avenue, Lincolnwood (Chicago), Illinois 60712-1975 U.S.A.
Copyright © 2001 by Daniella Chace
Printed in the United States of America
International Standard Book Number: 0-8092-9709-4

01 02 03 04 05 06 MV 19 18 17 16 15 14 13 12 11 10 9 8 7 6 5 4 3 2 1

Contents

Chapter 3: Salads

Chapter 4: Soups and Stews

Chapter 5: Sauces, Gravies, and Dressings

Chapter 6: Fish, Seafood, and Sea Vegetables

Chapter 7: Vegetables

Chapter 8: Desserts

Chapter 9: Smoothies and Cold Drinks

Chapter 10: Hot Drinks

Acknowledgments

I would like to thank the following friends and family for their contributions, ideas, and kitchen tips: Linda Hestag, Linda Landkammer, Dr. Bruce Milliman, Gary Boyer, Bobbie and Dick Boyer, and Merrilee Gomez. I would also like to thank Ann Wambach for her thorough copyediting.

Introduction

You are about to embark on a culinary adventure in which I hope you will discover new and healthful ways to prepare old favorite dishes as well as some unusual and medicinally powerful foods.

Many of you may have already read the counterpart to this book entitled *What to Eat if You Have Heart Disease* (Contemporary Books, 1998). In that book you will find the what, how, and why of heart disease. What is atherosclerosis, and how did it hurt my heart? What is cholesterol, and why is mine so high? What is saturated fat, and how did it end up in my arteries? In its chapters you will find the anatomy of heart disease, a crash course in the biochemistry of fat, and an explanation of the basis of most cardiovascular disease— atherosclerosis. The book also discusses other contributors to cardiovascular disease: some familiar, such as hypertension, and others that may be new to you, such as homocysteinemia and syndrome X. Although this cookbook can be used on its own, you will have a more comprehensive understanding of heart disease if you read *What to Eat if You Have Heart Disease*.

To get you started, here are a few tips. You will be introduced to many ingredients that have profound benefits in the treatment and prevention of heart disease. Each recipe uses whole, nongenetically altered foods to ensure maximum nutrients and phytochemicals. Genetically altered foods should be avoided because they contain higher residues of pesticides and herbicides than organic foods. It was recently discovered that genetically altered soybeans, for example, do not contain the phytochemicals that organic soybeans do. These phytochemicals have important medicinal properties, which help bones absorb calcium, inhibit tumor growth, reduce menopausal symptoms, and reduce cholesterol levels.

Organic foods have not been genetically altered. When you buy foods that are organic, local, and seasonal, you ensure maximum nutrients and the natural medicinal potential of that food. Always buy whole, unprocessed foods without added chemicals, coloring, preservatives, sugars, or sodium. Use only real ingredients such as real vanilla, not imitation, and real maple syrup, etc.

Organic canola oil is preferred for cooking because of its fat composition and its ability to withstand high temperatures. Extra-virgin olive oil is the most healthful choice with the best flavor for food preparation. Buy oils that have been extracted with a cold press method to avoid chemical process residue. For salad dressings and recipes that do not include heating, flax oil is used for its essential fatty acid content.

I recommend high-quality ingredients such as sea salt, which has a higher mineral concentration than table salt; low-sodium tamari that adds flavor without the sodium of soy sauce; and organic soy products such as organic tofu and organic soy milk.

Nutritional yeast is used in many recipes for its rich, cheesy flavor and high concentrations of minerals and B vitamins. Most of us do not get enough of the water-soluble B vitamins, but for those who are trying to reduce their homocysteine levels, these nutrients are an integral part of the treatment. Therefore, I have included foods rich in the homocysteine-reducing nutrients B_6, B_{12}, and folic acid in many recipes.

Blood-sugar regulation is critical for those with diabetes and hypoglycemia, and it is also important for those with syndrome X. To help stabilize blood sugar the recipes include legumes, high-fiber vegetables and grains, and the noncarbohydrate, all-natural sweetener stevia.

Soy foods have been included for their blood-sugar-regulating capacity as well as their ability to lower cholesterol. The recipes are low in fat and cholesterol and are generally low in calories.

I recommend that you use filtered water for drinking and cooking, especially when cooking beans, since minerals in tap water may toughen beans and keep them from cooking thoroughly.

When shopping for ingredients keep these tips in mind and stock your cupboards with the following basics. Buy your favorite whole grains (such as millet, quinoa, or brown rice) and dried beans in bulk so you'll always have some on hand. They will last for months in a cool dry place. Keep extra-virgin olive oil, canola oil, and flaxseed oil in the refrigerator, and they will last for months. Twice a week buy fresh, local, seasonal produce and throw it out as soon as it starts to deteriorate because it loses its nutritional value.

Remember that every step you take to eat better is a step toward optimal health. Most of all I hope these recipes will delight your palate while they heal your heart.

Daniella Chace

THE WHAT TO EAT
IF YOU HAVE HEART DISEASE

COOKBOOK

I

Breakfast

Muesli Breakfast Cereal

⌐◦ *Makes 12 servings*

This recipe has been adapted from Dr. Bruce Milliman's muesli recipe.

½ pound rolled oats
½ pound oat bran
¼ pound lecithin granules
¼ pound flaxseed, ground in a coffee grinder
⅛ pound raw pumpkin seeds
¼ pound filberts (hazelnuts)
⅛ pound pecans
6 ounces wheat germ
3 cups juice (apple or raspberry)
3 cups organic soy milk
3 cups plain unsweetened yogurt
3 cups blackberries or raspberries, *or* 3 cups chopped
   apple or pear

1. In a large bowl or paper bag, combine the oats, oat bran, lecithin, flaxseed, pumpkin seeds, nuts, and wheat germ.
2. For each individual serving soak ¼ cup muesli in ¼ cup juice for ½ hour before serving.
3. For each individual serving add ¼ cup soy milk, ¼ cup yogurt, and ¼ cup berries or chopped apple or pear and serve.
4. Store unused muesli in plastic bags or covered containers in the freezer.

PreparationTip: The hazelnuts and pecans can be dry roasted in a skillet for a nuttier flavor. Pour nuts into a dry skillet, no oil, and roast over medium heat until nuts begin to brown.

♥ HEART-HEALTHY TIP: This recipe is loaded with heart-healthy ingredients. The oats and bran contain fiber for improved digestion and blood-sugar maintenance, the flaxseeds provide omega-3 fatty acids, and the wheat germ is rich in vitamin E. The hazelnuts contain vitamin E which has been shown to decrease low-density lipoprotein (LDL) oxidation, and several population studies have suggested that people who eat foods higher in vitamin E are at less risk for heart disease.

NUTRITIONAL INFORMATION PER SERVING

Calories 360	Fiber 8g
Carbohydrate 26g	Cholesterol 0mg
Protein 13g	Sodium 10mg
Fat 22g	

Sweet Onion and Potato Pancakes

~ Makes 4 servings

1 cup organic soy milk
½ cup steel-cut oats (not instant)
1 cup instant potato flakes
2 medium carrots, pared and shredded
2 onions, grated
¼ cup nutritional yeast flakes
½ teaspoon sea salt
½ teaspoon garlic powder
Pepper, to taste

1. Boil milk in a saucepan. Remove from heat, and stir in the oats.
2. Cover and let stand for 5 minutes.
3. Stir in the remaining ingredients, mixing thoroughly.
4. Form into 16 thin patties.
5. Heat a nonstick or oiled skillet and add patties. Sauté for about 10 minutes on each side until brown.

Preparation Tip: A variety of different root vegetables can be used in place of, or in combination with, the potatoes in this recipe. If oil is needed for sautéing, canola oil is a good choice because it adds little flavor of its own and won't burn easily.

♥ **HEART-HEALTHY TIP:** Arginine, an amino acid found in oats, helps the arteries to relax, reducing the risk of heart disease, hypertension, and stroke.

NUTRITIONAL INFORMATION PER SERVING

Calories 360

Carbohydrate 69g

Protein 14g

Fat 2.5g

Fiber 12g

Cholesterol 0mg

Sodium 250mg

Nutty Scones

....

∽ Makes 12 scones

1 cup whole wheat pastry flour

1 cup cornmeal

2 tablespoons unbleached cane sugar

2 teaspoons baking powder

½ teaspoon baking soda

¾ teaspoon sea salt

1 cup ground nuts (walnuts, almonds, or sesame seeds)

6 tablespoons butter, chilled

¾ cup organic soy milk

1 tablespoon fresh lemon juice

1. Preheat oven to 425°F.

2. In a large bowl, combine flour, cornmeal, sugar, baking powder, baking soda, and salt.

3. Grind nuts in a coffee grinder or food processor and add to dry ingredients.

4. Shred butter with a cheese grater into dry ingredients and mix well into a coarse meal.

5. Add the soy milk and lemon juice and mix well into a sticky dough.

6. Roll dough into a log and slice into 1-inch rounds. Transfer the slices to a baking sheet and bake for 15 minutes.

7. Transfer to a wire rack to cool.

♥ **Heart-Healthy Tip:** There is some evidence that vitamin E, found in nuts, may help to prevent second heart attacks. Vitamin E reduces the platelet aggregation that initiates myocardial infarction. One study found that it helped to prevent the reclosing of coronary arteries opened by angioplasty. Nuts are also a great source of zinc and calcium.

NUTRITIONAL INFORMATION PER SCONE

Calories 220

Carbohydrate 20g

Protein 5g

Fat 13g

Fiber 2g

Cholesterol 15mg

Sodium 130mg

Breakfast Muffins

⁓ Makes 15 muffins

1 cup low-fat ricotta cheese
½ cup unsweetened applesauce
½ cup prune puree
2 tablespoons flaxseed oil
1 egg
2 teaspoons vanilla extract
1¼ cups whole wheat flour
½ cup wheat germ
1 teaspoon baking powder
1 teaspoon nutmeg
1 teaspoon allspice
1 cup shredded zucchini or carrot
¼ cup chopped apple
¼ cup raisins or currants
¼ cup pumpkin seeds

1. In a large bowl, combine ricotta, applesauce, prune puree, and oil.
2. Stir in egg and vanilla.
3. In separate bowl, combine flour, wheat germ, baking powder, nutmeg, and allspice. Add to batter and blend well.
4. Add zucchini, apples, raisins, and pumpkin seeds.
5. Spoon batter into nonstick or oiled muffin tins.
6. Bake at 350°F for 20 to 25 minutes, or until golden brown.

♥ **HEART-HEALTHY TIP:** Wheat germ is rich in the mineral magnesium, which reduces vasoconstriction and reduces blood pressure and platelet stickiness.

NUTRITIONAL INFORMATION PER MUFFIN

Calories 130

Carbohydrate 16g

Protein 6g

Fat 5g

Fiber 2g

Cholesterol 15mg

Sodium 40mg

Breakfast Smoothie

~ *Makes 1 serving*

1 cup organic soy milk
1 frozen banana
1 tablespoon ground flaxseed
½ cup frozen strawberries
1 tablespoon unbleached cane sugar

1. Freeze the banana ahead of time by peeling it and placing it into a plastic bag in the freezer. Do not freeze with the peel intact; it is very difficult to remove once frozen.
2. Combine all ingredients in a blender.
3. Blend until smooth.

Preparation Tip: Peel organic bananas and place them in a Ziploc bag in the freezer. Frozen bananas are a tasty potassium- and fiber-rich addition to any smoothie.

NUTRITIONAL INFORMATION PER SERVING

Calories 400
Carbohydrate 66g
Protein 10g
Fat 11g

Fiber 7g
Cholesterol 0mg
Sodium 150mg

Scrambled Tofu

....

~ *Makes 2 servings*

½ sweet onion, chopped
1 clove garlic, chopped
1 tablespoon extra-virgin olive oil
½ pound firm organic tofu, crumbled
1 tablespoon low-sodium tamari
¼ teaspoon turmeric powder
¼ cup chopped fresh basil leaves
3 tablespoons nutritional yeast
¼ cup grated organic soy Parmesan cheese

1. Sauté the onion and garlic in the olive oil until the onion becomes translucent.
2. Crumble the tofu into the pan and sprinkle tamari and turmeric over the top. Stirring frequently, continue cooking over medium heat. The turmeric should give the tofu a yellow egglike color.
3. Continue to cook the tofu until it begins to brown.
4. Add the basil leaves, nutritional yeast, and Parmesan cheese. Cover and heat for another 5 minutes.
5. Serve hot.

♥ **HEART-HEALTHY TIP:** Nutritional yeast is a rich source of the B vitamins. A quarter cup of nutritional yeast contains 8 mg of vitamin B_1, 3 mg of B_2, 26 mg of B_3, 2 mg of B_6, and about 1,500 micrograms of folate.

NUTRITIONAL INFORMATION PER SERVING

Calories 280	Fiber 10g
Carbohydrate 18g	Cholesterol 0mg
Protein 24g	Sodium 590mg
Fat 12g	

Tofu Pancakes

....

Makes 10 pancakes

1 ½ cups milk or soy milk

2 egg whites

½ pound silken organic tofu

1 tablespoon organic canola oil

2 tablespoons maple syrup

1 teaspoon baking powder

2 teaspoons vanilla extract

¼ teaspoon sea salt

1 cup whole wheat flour

1. In a blender or food processor, combine all ingredients and blend until smooth.
2. Pour onto a nonstick or lightly oiled hot skillet, making 10 pancakes.
3. Cook pancakes on both sides until golden brown.
4. Serve hot.

Preparation Tip: Cut recipe in half for two people.

NUTRITIONAL INFORMATION PER PANCAKE
....

Calories 110

Carbohydrate 15g

Protein 4g

Fat 3g

Fiber 1g

Cholesterol 0mg

Sodium 95mg

Tofu French Toast

4 egg whites
1 pound silken organic tofu
½ teaspoon cinnamon
½ teaspoon sea salt
¼ cup maple syrup
2 teaspoons vanilla extract
6 slices whole-grain bread

1. Combine egg whites, tofu, cinnamon, salt, maple syrup, and vanilla in a blender and process until smooth.
2. Coat each slice of bread in egg mixture and place in a hot nonstick or lightly oiled skillet.
3. Cook over medium heat until brown. Turn over each slice and brown.
4. Serve with maple syrup.

Preparation Tip: Many tofu packages contain more than one pound of tofu. In this case you will have left-over tofu, which can be placed back in its original packing, covered with water, and stored in the refrigerator for up to three days.

NUTRITIONAL INFORMATION PER SLICE

Calories 150
Carbohydrate 21g
Protein 11g
Fat 3g

Fiber 4g
Cholesterol 0mg
Sodium 200mg

Eggless Waffles

Makes 4 waffles

2 cups organic soy milk
4 tablespoons ground flaxseed
2 tablespoons maple syrup
1 teaspoon vanilla extract
⅛ teaspoon nutmeg
⅛ teaspoon cinnamon
¼ cup toasted chopped pecans
2 cups whole wheat flour
1 teaspoon baking soda
2 teaspoons baking powder
⅛ teaspoon sea salt

1. In a blender, combine soy milk, flaxseed, maple syrup, vanilla, nutmeg, cinnamon, and pecans. Process until mixed.
2. In large bowl, combine flour, baking soda, baking powder, and salt.
3. Add the wet ingredients to the bowl and mix well.
4. Pour into a hot oiled waffle iron.
5. When steam stops rising from the iron, open lid. Waffle should be golden brown. Use a fork to remove waffle from iron.
6. Serve hot.

Preparation Tip: Use canola oil in waffle iron because it handles heat well.

♥ **HEART-HEALTHY TIP:** Flaxseed and flaxseed oil contain essential fatty acids which provide the linoleic and linolenic acid necessary for the proper development of nerve cells, cellular membranes, and prostaglandin production.

NUTRITIONAL INFORMATION PER WAFFLE

Calories 400

Carbohydrate 61g

Protein 12g

Fat 12g

Fiber 8g

Cholesterol 0mg

Sodium 420mg

Maple Syrup

⤳ Makes 6 servings

¼ teaspoon guar gum
⅓ cup water
1 teaspoon maple flavoring
1 tablespoon maple syrup
1 pinch stevia extract powder *or* 3 drops liquid extract
¼ teaspoon hazelnut oil

1. Place all ingredients together in a blender or food processor and blend until smooth.
2. Serve over pancakes or waffles.

♥ HEART-HEALTHY TIP: This low-calorie, low-fat, low-sugar version of maple syrup is delicious and rich without the unhealthy addition of synthetic sweeteners.

NUTRITIONAL INFORMATION PER SERVING

Calories 0
Carbohydrate 1g
Protein 0g
Fat 0g

Fiber 0g
Cholesterol 0mg
Sodium 0mg

2

Appetizers and Snacks

Edamame

....

⁓ Makes 2 servings

1 pound organic young green soybeans (shelled)
¼ teaspoon sea salt

1. Steam soybeans in a bamboo steamer or a covered saucepan with at least 1 inch of water for 5 to 8 minutes.
2. Salt and serve hot.

Preparation Tip: The young green soybeans are generally sold in plastic bags in the freezer department of natural-food stores or Asian grocery markets. They can be purchased in their pod or shelled. The easiest way to eat soybeans in the shell is to hold the pod and pop the beans into your mouth. Kids love edamame in the pod.

♥ **HEART-HEALTHY TIP:** Soybeans help reduce cholesterol levels. Soybeans are rich in saponins, substances that resemble cholesterol in their chemical makeup. Saponins are believed to lower cholesterol either by blocking cholesterol absorption or by causing more cholesterol to be excreted from the body.

NUTRITIONAL INFORMATION PER SERVING
....

Calories 340

Carbohydrate 25g

Protein 28g

Fat 15g

Fiber 10g

Cholesterol 0mg

Sodium 1,200mg

Miso Soup

....

Makes 1 serving

1 cup hot water
1 tablespoon miso paste
¼ scallion, sliced

1. Combine hot water and miso paste in a mug.
2. Add scallion rounds to taste.

♥ **HEART-HEALTHY TIP:** Soy foods such as miso contain isoflavones. These substances are unique to soy foods and lower total serum cholesterol, LDL cholesterol, and increase the high-density lipoprotein to low-density lipoprotein ratio. Isoflavones have also been shown to possess antioxidant properties.

NUTRITIONAL INFORMATION PER SERVING

Calories 50

Carbohydrate 7g

Protein 3g

Fat 1g

Fiber 2g

Cholesterol 0mg

Sodium 640mg

Bean and Salsa Dip

⌇ Makes 4 servings

1 cup dried black beans
4 cups water
4 corn tortillas
1 cup salsa

1. Cook black beans with water in a pressure cooker for 30 minutes.
2. Toast the tortillas in a toaster or toaster-oven until crisp. If you don't have a toaster, the tortillas can also be crisped in a skillet on the stove; however, a toaster uses the least amount of energy.
3. When the beans are cooked, strain and rinse.
4. Combine the salsa with the beans and serve with wedges of the toasted corn tortillas used for dipping.

Preparation Tip: Prepare the corn tortillas as directed in the recipe Cheesy Tortillas (see Index) for a tasty vitamin- and mineral-rich addition to this snack.

NUTRITIONAL INFORMATION PER SERVING

Calories 240
Carbohydrate 42g
Protein 15g
Fat 1.5g

Fiber 10g
Cholesterol 0mg
Sodium 530mg

Guacamole

....

~ *Makes 4 servings*

1 large ripe avocado, minced
2 ripe tomatoes, minced
1 teaspoon garlic powder *or* 3 cloves fresh garlic, minced
3 tablespoons fresh lemon juice
1 teaspoon balsamic vinegar
1 scallion, minced
¼ red onion, minced

1. Mash all ingredients together in a large bowl.
2. Serve with baked corn chips or raw vegetables.

♥ **HEART-HEALTHY TIP:** Tomatoes contain vitamin C, which is necessary for collagen formation. Collagen gives skin a smooth healthy look and is involved in wound healing. Humans are one of the few mammals that are unable to make vitamin C and must get it through the diet. Other mammals are able to manufacture their own supplies as needed.

NUTRITIONAL INFORMATION PER SERVING
....

Calories 80

Carbohydrate 9g

Protein 1g

Fat 4.5g

Fiber 2g

Cholesterol 0mg

Sodium 130mg

Sesame Breadsticks

Makes 32 breadsticks

1 pound silken organic tofu
4 tablespoons butter, softened
1 ½ teaspoons sea salt
2 teaspoons dried basil
¼ teaspoon cayenne pepper
2 ½ teaspoons baking powder
1 cup toasted sesame seeds
2 ½ cups whole wheat flour

1. Preheat oven to 375°F.
2. In a blender or food processor, combine tofu, butter, salt, basil, cayenne, and baking powder. Process until smooth.
3. In a dry skillet, toast the sesame seeds over medium heat until browned. Watch them closely and stir often as the oils in the seeds will burn easily.
4. In a large bowl, combine sesame seeds and whole wheat flour.
5. Pour tofu batter into dry ingredients and use an electric mixer, or knead by hand until smooth.
6. Roll into 5-inch-long sticks. Place on a nonstick or lightly oiled baking sheet.
7. Bake for 30 to 35 minutes. Baking time may vary depending on the thickness of the sticks.
8. Serve warm or cool.

Preparation Tip: Add freshly grated Parmesan cheese, herbs, and spices to the dough to alter the flavor as desired. Also nutritional yeast can be added to give the sticks a cheesy flavor while adding vitamins, minerals, and fiber.

♥ **HEART-HEALTHY TIP:** Sesame seeds are a rich source of copper and magnesium, which protect against heart disease, hypertension, and stroke.

NUTRITIONAL INFORMATION PER BREADSTICK

Calories 110

Carbohydrate 14g

Protein 4g

Fat 4.5g

Fiber 1g

Cholesterol 5mg

Sodium 115mg

Open-Face Avocado Melts

~ Makes 2 servings

1 ounce Parmesan cheese, sliced thin
4 slices whole-grain bread
1 ripe avocado, sliced
1 ripe roma tomato, sliced

1. Place cheese slices on bread and toast under broiler until the cheese begins to soften.
2. Add the avocado and tomato slices.
3. Salt and pepper to taste and serve.

♥ **HEART-HEALTHY TIP:** One avocado contains 11 grams of fiber, 1,378 mg of potassium, 25 mg of calcium, 89 mg of magnesium, and healthy monounsaturated fats.

NUTRITIONAL INFORMATION PER SERVING

Calories 310

Carbohydrate 31g

Protein 12g

Fat 15g

Fiber 6g

Cholesterol 10mg

Sodium 590mg

Tofu Meatballs

~ *Makes 8 servings*

1 pound silken organic tofu, crumbled

2 eggs

½ cup whole wheat bread crumbs

2 tablespoons low-sodium tamari

½ teaspoon onion salt

½ teaspoon Italian seasoning

1 teaspoon minced fresh garlic

¼ cup grated Parmesan cheese

1 tablespoon onion flakes

¼ teaspoon pepper

¼ teaspoon nutmeg

1 tablespoon extra-virgin olive oil

1. Combine all ingredients, except oil, in bowl and mix well.
2. Form into 1-inch balls.
3. Heat oil in large skillet and add tofu balls. Sauté over medium-low heat, turning occasionally, until browned.

Preparation Tip: Make small meatballs and serve them with toothpicks on a plate with marinara sauce for dipping.

NUTRITIONAL INFORMATION PER SERVING

Calories 90

Carbohydrate 5g

Protein 7g

Fat 4.5g

Fiber 1g

Cholesterol 55mg

Sodium 380mg

Cheesy Tortillas

⌐ *Makes 2 servings*

2 small corn tortillas
⅛ teaspoon butter
1 tablespoon nutritional yeast flakes

1. Toast the tortillas in a toaster just the way you would toast bread.
2. When they pop up, remove from toaster and immediately wipe one side of each tortilla with butter. It won't take much to cover them when they are hot.
3. Sprinkle tortillas with nutritional yeast and eat them while they are still soft.

♥ **HEART-HEALTHY TIP:** A tablespoon of nutritional yeast contains about 270 mg of potassium, 3 mg of iron, 45 mg of calcium, 30 mg of magnesium, 1 mg of zinc, 5 mg of protein, and 5 mg of fiber, as well as concentrations of all the B vitamins.

NUTRITIONAL INFORMATION PER SERVING

Calories 100

Carbohydrate 17g

Protein 7g

Fat 1g

Fiber 6g

Cholesterol 0mg

Sodium 45mg

Soy Nuts

⚘ Makes 4 servings

1 cup dried soybeans
1 quart water

1. Cover beans with water and soak for about 3 hours.
2. Strain and rinse beans.
3. Preheat oven to 350°F.
4. Spread beans out onto a baking sheet and bake for 1 hour, stirring frequently until well browned.
5. Store unused portion in an airtight container for up to 2 weeks.

NUTRITIONAL INFORMATION PER SERVING

Calories 230

Carbohydrate 15g

Protein 19g

Fat 11g

Fiber 3g

Cholesterol 0mg

Sodium 35mg

Popcorn with Nutritional Yeast

Makes 4 servings

¼ cup nutritional yeast
¼ teaspoon black pepper
½ teaspoon garlic powder
¼ teaspoon chili powder
½ teaspoon sea salt
3 tablespoons organic canola oil
¼ cup popcorn kernels

1. In a small bowl, thoroughly mix the yeast, black pepper, garlic powder, chili powder, and salt. Set aside.
2. Heat the oil in a saucepan and add corn kernels, cover, and heat over medium-high heat. Within a few minutes the kernels will have popped.
3. Remove the lid, pour the popcorn into a bowl, and add seasoning mix. It is important to move quickly when kernels are done popping. Sprinkle the toppings on while the kernels are still steaming hot, the steam will help the toppings stick to the kernels; or pour the toppings and the popcorn into a paper bag, folding down the top, and shake the bag vigorously to coat the popcorn evenly.

♥ **HEART-HEALTHY TIP:** The Framingham Heart Study found that increased homocysteine levels are associated with increased risk of heart attack, atherosclerosis, and stroke. By increasing pyridoxine (B_6), vitamin cobalamin (B_{12}), and folate levels, serum homocysteine can be reduced. This treatment may slow the progress of the disease and decrease the likelihood of future vascular events. Nutritional yeast is rich in the B vitamins, B_6, B_{12}, and folate.

NUTRITIONAL INFORMATION PER SERVING

Calories 160

Carbohydrate 9g

Protein 6g

Fat 11g

Fiber 5g

Cholesterol 0mg

Sodium 290mg

Sweet Corn Bread

~ Makes 12 servings

2½ teaspoons baking powder

¼ teaspoon sea salt

2 cups blue or yellow cornmeal

Pinch of cayenne pepper (optional)

2 egg whites

3 tablespoons extra-virgin olive or canola oil

1 cup soy milk

1 tablespoon maple syrup

1–2 tablespoons seeded, minced fresh jalapeño pepper

2 cups corn kernels, fresh or frozen

1. Preheat oven to 425°F.
2. Lightly oil a 9-inch square baking dish or muffin tins.
3. In a large bowl, combine baking powder, sea salt, cornmeal, and cayenne pepper, if desired; blend well.
4. In a medium bowl whip together egg whites until fluffy. Then add oil, soy milk, maple syrup, jalapeño, and corn.
5. Pour liquid ingredients into large bowl with the dry ingredients and fold together.
6. Pour into prepared pan or muffin tins and bake for 20 to 25 minutes.

NUTRITIONAL INFORMATION PER SERVING

Calories 140

Carbohydrate 23g

Protein 3g

Fat 4.5g

Fiber 2g

Cholesterol 0mg

Sodium 70mg

3

Salads

Exotic Green Tea Salad

~ Makes 2 servings

4 cloves garlic, sliced thin

1 teaspoon sesame oil

2 tablespoons green tea leaves

1 ½ tablespoons fish sauce

2 tablespoons fresh lemon juice

2 tablespoons low-sodium tamari

1 tablespoon shredded fresh gingerroot

¼ jalapeño pepper, seeded and minced

2 tablespoons toasted shredded coconut

4 tablespoons chopped roasted peanuts

1 tablespoon toasted sesame seeds

1 cup shredded romaine lettuce or raw spinach

1 fresh tomato, chopped

2 lemon wedges

1. Sauté garlic in sesame oil just until brown.
2. In a small bowl, combine tea leaves, fish sauce, lemon juice, tamari, gingerroot, and jalapeño.
3. Add the sautéed garlic.
4. Allow this sauce to stand for 15 to 20 minutes.
5. Stir in the coconut, peanuts, and sesame seeds.
6. In a large bowl, toss romaine and tomato together.
7. Add the sauce and toss all together.
8. Serve with lemon wedges on the side.

♥ **HEART-HEALTHY TIP:** Green tea leaves are a good source of vitamin K when eaten rather than used to make tea.

NUTRITIONAL INFORMATION PER SERVING

Calories 230

Carbohydrate 17g

Protein 10g

Fat 14g

Fiber 5g

Cholesterol 0mg

Sodium 1,320mg

Blue Cheese and Pear Salad

Makes 4 servings

¼ cup coarsely chopped pecans
¼ teaspoon cinnamon
¼ teaspoon nutmeg
½ teaspoon unbleached (turbinado) sugar
¼ teaspoon sea salt
2 tablespoons flaxseed oil
2 tablespoons fresh lime juice
1 tablespoon honey
1 teaspoon grated fresh gingerroot
¼ teaspoon freshly ground pepper
4 Bartlett pears, cored and sliced
2 bunches watercress, rinsed and chopped
½ cup dried currants
2 ounces blue cheese, crumbled

1. Combine pecans, cinnamon, nutmeg, sugar, and salt in a paper bag and fold bag closed. Shake bag vigorously to coat the nuts.
2. Spread nuts out on a cookie sheet and bake at 250°F for 10 minutes. Set aside.
3. In large bowl, combine flaxseed oil, lime juice, honey, gingerroot, and pepper.
4. Add pear slices and toss until well coated.
5. Place watercress on salad plates. Arrange pear slices on each plate and spoon remaining dressing over each.
6. Garnish the top of each salad with currants, blue cheese, and roasted nuts.

Preparation Tip: Walnuts are also delicious in this recipe and can be used in place of the pecans.

NUTRITIONAL INFORMATION PER SERVING

Calories 340

Carbohydrate 45g

Protein 4g

Fat 16g

Fiber 6g

Cholesterol 15mg

Sodium 170mg

Asian Tofu Salad

~ *Makes 4 servings*

½ pound firm organic tofu, crumbled
3 tablespoons low-sodium tamari
1 tablespoon fresh lemon juice
1 tablespoon extra-virgin olive oil
1 red pepper, sliced
1 yellow pepper, sliced
1 cup mung bean sprouts
½ cup roasted peanuts
¼ cup sesame seeds
2 cups shredded red cabbage
2 cups sliced napa cabbage
1 scallion, sliced
¼ cup minced red onion

1. Marinate tofu in tamari, lemon juice, and olive oil while preparing other ingredients.
2. In a large salad bowl, combine peppers, sprouts, peanuts, sesame seeds, cabbage, scallion, and red onion.
3. Dress with your choice of low-fat, low-sodium salad dressing or sprinkle the top with lemon juice, balsamic vinegar, and a tablespoon of extra-virgin olive oil.

♥ **HEART-HEALTHY TIP:** Nuts are an important part of a heart-healthy diet. They are loaded with the antioxidant vitamin E. Research suggests that vitamin E supplements may help to slow or even reverse ischemic heart disease.

NUTRITIONAL INFORMATION PER SERVING

Calories 240

Carbohydrate 14g

Protein 12g

Fat 14g

Fiber 6g

Cholesterol 0mg

Sodium 640mg

Spinach Caesar Salad

Makes 4 servings

1 bunch spinach, washed and chopped
3 tablespoons flaxseed oil
¼ cup fresh lemon juice
¼ teaspoon sea salt
4 cloves garlic, minced
¼ cup freshly grated Parmesan cheese

1. Wash spinach leaves well and spin dry or set out on a clean towel to dry.
2. Combine flaxseed oil, lemon juice, salt, and garlic in a large bowl.
3. Chop spinach and toss with the dressing.
4. Add Parmesan cheese and serve.

♥ **Heart-Healthy Tip:** Garlic contains sulfur compounds that act as natural antibiotics, helping stave off bacterial and viral infections.

NUTRITIONAL INFORMATION PER SERVING

Calories 100
Carbohydrate 2g
Protein 3g
Fat 9g

Fiber 1g
Cholesterol 5mg
Sodium 260mg

Greek Salad

....

~ *Makes 8 servings*

4 large cucumbers, peeled and sliced thin
4 ripe tomatoes, sliced
½ cup sliced red onion
3 cloves garlic, minced
¼ cup balsamic vinegar
2 tablespoons flaxseed oil
2 tablespoons fresh lemon juice

1. Combine all ingredients in a large bowl.
2. Serve immediately or chill in covered container up to 2 hours.

♥ **HEART-HEALTHY TIP:** Flaxseed oil is widely available and inexpensive. It is a rich source of omega-3 and omega-6 fats as well as carotene and vitamin E.

NUTRITIONAL INFORMATION PER SERVING

Calories 80
Carbohydrate 8g
Protein 2g
Fat 4g

Fiber 2g
Cholesterol 0mg
Sodium 10mg

Red Sesame Salad

⁓ Makes 4 servings

1 cup shredded raw beets
2 cups shredded carrot
¼ cup chopped red onion
1 teaspoon grated fresh gingerroot
2 tablespoons low-sodium tamari
2 tablespoons fresh lemon juice
2 tablespoons sesame seeds

1. Combine all ingredients in a bowl and serve.

♥ **HEART-HEALTHY TIP:** Sesame seeds contain alpha-linolenic acid, high levels of which are associated with lower risk of stroke.

NUTRITIONAL INFORMATION PER SERVING

Calories 120
Carbohydrate 21g
Protein 4g
Fat 2.5g

Fiber 6g
Cholesterol 0mg
Sodium 390mg

Sweet Corn Salad

....

∼ *Makes 6 servings*

½ cup balsamic vinegar
2 tablespoons flaxseed oil
1 teaspoon chili powder
½ teaspoon sea salt
4 cups fresh or frozen corn kernels, thawed
½ cup chopped walnuts
½ red bell pepper, chopped
½ green bell pepper, chopped
¼ cup chopped Italian parsley
2 scallions, chopped
½ cup raisins
¼ cup crumbled blue cheese (optional)

1. In a large mixing bowl, combine vinegar, oil, chili powder, and salt. Add corn, walnuts, bell peppers, parsley, scallions, raisins, and blue cheese, if desired.
2. Toss and serve.

Preparation Tip: Buy only flaxseed oil that is certified organic, unrefined, fresh-pressed, and made by a reputable company such as Omega Nutrition or Arrowhead Mills.

NUTRITIONAL INFORMATION PER SERVING
....

Calories 270	Fiber 4g
Carbohydrate 35g	Cholesterol 0mg
Protein 6g	Sodium 210mg
Fat 11g	

Szechuan Pepper Salad

Makes 2 servings

1 bunch spinach, washed and chopped
1 avocado, sliced
½ ruby red grapefruit, peeled and chopped
1 tablespoon Szechuan peppers
2 tablespoons fresh lemon juice
2 tablespoons balsamic vinegar
2 cloves garlic, peeled and minced
2 tablespoons low-sodium tamari
2 tablespoons flaxseed oil or extra-virgin olive oil

1. Combine spinach, avocado, and grapefruit in a large bowl.
2. Grind Szechuan peppers with a pestle and mortar to release flavors.
3. In a small bowl, combine, ground Szechuan peppers, lemon juice, balsamic vinegar, garlic, tamari, and oil.
4. Mix dressing well and toss into salad.

♥ HEART-HEALTHY TIP: Flaxseed oil is a good source of essential fatty acids. EFAs improve vasodilation and nerve conduction and reduce incidence of microangiopathy and neuropathy.

NUTRITIONAL INFORMATION PER SERVING

Calories 290	Fiber 5g
Carbohydrate 15g	Cholesterol 0mg
Protein 5g	Sodium 660mg
Fat 23g	

Tofu Croutons

〜 *Makes 6 servings*

1 pound frozen organic tofu, thawed, rinsed, and
   squeezed dry
1 teaspoon dried basil
1 teaspoon dried oregano
¼ teaspoon sea salt

1. Cut tofu into ½-inch squares and place on a baking
   sheet.
2. Bake at 350°F for 10 to 15 minutes, turning as needed
   to brown.
3. Place in a paper bag with herbs and shake until well
   coated.
4. Serve with salads and soups

♥ **HEART-HEALTHY TIP:** The amount and types of
polyunsaturated acids you eat can alter the way your body
handles chylomicrons. High levels of chylomicron remnants in
the blood are believed to promote atherosclerosis. The
remnants are small enough to slip between the endothelial
cells and enter the intimal layer where they are stored as
cholesterol. To reduce the numbers of chylomicrons
circulating in the blood, eat less fat and more soy protein.

NUTRITIONAL INFORMATION PER SERVING

Calories 50

Carbohydrate 2g

Protein 5g

Fat 2.5g

Fiber 1g

Cholesterol 0mg

Sodium 125mg

Garlic Curry Tuna Salad

Makes 2 servings

4 slices whole-grain bread
1 6-ounce can tuna fish, water packed, drained
¼ cup minced walnuts
½ cup minced cilantro
2 cloves garlic, minced
1 tablespoon fresh lemon juice
1 tablespoon curry powder
1 tablespoon mayonnaise

1. Toast bread.
2. In a large bowl, combine tuna, walnuts, cilantro, garlic, lemon juice, curry powder, and mayonnaise.
3. Spread the tuna salad on toast and enjoy.

♥ **HEART-HEALTHY TIP:** Fish oil has reduced the incidence of fatal heart attacks in those with heart disease and slowed the progression of atherosclerosis. Daily intake of fish oil helps reduce triglyceride levels.

NUTRITIONAL INFORMATION PER SERVING

Calories 380

Carbohydrate 27g

Protein 22g

Fat 20g

Fiber 4g

Cholesterol 10mg

Sodium 450mg

4

Soups and Stews

East Indian Stew

....

~ *Makes 6 servings*

1 tablespoon peanut oil or ghee
2 tablespoons mustard seeds
2 teaspoons cumin seeds
2 teaspoons fennel seeds
1 teaspoon coriander seeds
2 cups coarsely chopped onion
2 tablespoons finely minced fresh gingerroot
½–1 teaspoon crushed red pepper flakes
2 cups water
2 cups soy milk
1 15-ounce can diced tomatoes with liquid
1¼ cups red lentils
2 carrots, chopped
½ cup grated unsweetened dried coconut
½ teaspoon sea salt
1 cup chopped fresh cilantro

1. Heat oil in a large soup pot over medium heat.
2. Add mustard, cumin, fennel, and coriander seeds. Cover and heat until the seeds begin to pop, about 30 seconds. Turn off the heat and let sit, covered, until the seeds stop popping, about 1 minute.
3. Add the onion, gingerroot, and red pepper flakes. Sauté over medium-high heat for 1 minute, stirring frequently.
4. Add water, soy milk, and tomatoes with canning liquid and bring to a gentle boil. Reduce the heat to medium-low and add the lentils, carrots, and coconut. Cover and cook for 20 minutes, stirring occasionally.

5. Add the salt and cilantro and continue cooking for another 10 minutes.

6. Serve hot.

Preparation Tip: Ghee is an East Indian condiment. It is simply clarified butter that can be purchased at many grocery or specialty markets. It can also be made at home by melting butter and using a spoon to scoop off the froth that floats to the top. Clarifying the butter removes impurities and also raises its burning temperature.

♥ **HEART-HEALTHY TIP:** Carrots contain pectin, a soluble fiber, which is beneficial in blood-sugar regulation, removing metals and toxins in the digestive tract, and reducing cholesterol and triglyceride levels.

NUTRITIONAL INFORMATION PER SERVING

Calories 270

Carbohydrate 44g

Protein 14g

Fat 3.5g

Fiber 5g

Cholesterol 5mg

Sodium 270mg

Creamy Garlic Potato Soup

⁓ Makes 6 servings

2 cups cubed potato
4 cups water
2 cups chopped onion
2 leeks, chopped
5 cloves garlic, minced
½ tablespoon extra-virgin olive oil
3 tablespoons miso paste
¼ cup chopped fresh Italian parsley
½ teaspoon sea salt
¼ teaspoon red cracked pepper
1 cup plain soy milk
⅛ teaspoon black pepper

1. Boil potatoes in water until soft, about 20 minutes, and reserve the cooking water.
2. Sauté onion, leeks, and garlic in olive oil.
3. In a blender, combine 2 tablespoons miso paste, potatoes, and the cooking water (reserved in step one), and blend until desired consistency.
4. Return to soup pot; stir in parsley, sea salt, red pepper, soy milk, and black pepper.
5. Heat until almost boiling but do not boil, as the milk will curdle.
6. Garnish with a few sprigs of Italian parsley.

Preparation Tip: Use pressure cooker to speed up the cooking time for the potatoes.

♥ HEART-HEALTHY TIP: Genistein, a natural plant chemical found in soy foods such as miso, is an antioxidant that helps prevent free-radical damage.

NUTRITIONAL INFORMATION PER SERVING

Calories 120

Carbohydrate 21g

Protein 4g

Fat 2g

Fiber 2g

Cholesterol 0mg

Sodium 710mg

Carrot Soup

....

~ *Makes 4 servings*

4 cups water
2 cups chopped carrot
1 cup chopped onion
½ teaspoon black pepper
½ teaspoon garlic powder
¼ teaspoon sea salt
⅛ teaspoon savory
⅛ teaspoon cayenne pepper
1 tablespoon butter

1. Mix all ingredients in a medium saucepan and bring to a boil.
2. Reduce heat to a simmer and cook until carrots become soft.
3. Use a fork or wooden spoon to mash carrots slightly.
4. Salt and pepper to taste.

♥ **HEART-HEALTHY TIP:** Studies of large populations suggest that people who have a large intake of antioxidant nutrients have a 20 to 40 percent lower risk of developing heart disease. Beta-carotene is just one of many carotenoids with antioxidant properties.

NUTRITIONAL INFORMATION PER SERVING
....

Calories 100

Carbohydrate 15g

Protein 2g

Fat 3.5g

Fiber 4g

Cholesterol 10mg

Sodium 220mg

Potato and Corn Chowder

Makes 4 servings

4 large potatoes, cut into ½-inch cubes, skin left on

1 large onion, chopped

2 cups water

1 cube chicken or vegetable bouillon

2 teaspoons dried basil

½ teaspoon sea salt

¼ teaspoon pepper

1 14.5-ounce can cream-style corn

1 14-ounce can whole kernel corn, drained

1 cup plain organic soy milk

1. In a medium saucepan, combine the potatoes, onion, water, bouillon, basil, salt, and pepper.
2. Bring to a boil, reduce heat, and simmer until potatoes are tender, about 15 to 20 minutes. Remove pan from heat and stir in both cans of corn.
3. Pour two cups of the soup into a blender and briefly puree.
4. Return the pureed soup to the saucepan, stir in the soy milk and heat thoroughly over medium heat.
5. Add spices and seasonings to taste.

NUTRITIONAL INFORMATION PER SERVING

Calories 350	Fiber 8g
Carbohydrate 73g	Cholesterol 0mg
Protein 9g	Sodium 620mg
Fat 2.5g	

Khyber Stew

....

~ *Makes 6 servings*

3 tablespoons mustard seeds

2 teaspoons cumin seeds

2 teaspoons fennel seeds

1 teaspoon cardamom

1 tablespoon organic butter

2 cups chopped onion

3 tablespoons minced fresh gingerroot

1 teaspoon seeded and minced fresh chili pepper

2 cups vegetable broth or water

2 cups organic soy milk

1 15-ounce can stewed tomatoes

2 cups red lentils

3 carrots, chopped

½ teaspoon sea salt

1. In a large saucepan, heat mustard seed, cumin, fennel, and cardamom in butter. The mustard seeds will begin to pop within about 30 seconds.
2. Add onion, gingerroot, and chili pepper. Sauté for about 1 minute.
3. Add broth, soy milk, stewed tomatoes, lentils, carrots, and salt and cook covered for 30 to 40 minutes.
4. Serve hot.

NUTRITIONAL INFORMATION PER SERVING

Calories 370

Carbohydrate 57g

Protein 24g

Fat 5g

Fiber 22g

Cholesterol 5mg

Sodium 680mg

Ginger Miso Soup

~ *Makes 4 servings*

6 cups water

1 carrot, chopped

2 tablespoons minced fresh gingerroot

3 cups chopped napa cabbage, sliced thin

1 15-ounce can organic soybeans

¼ cup miso paste (e.g., barley or rice miso)

1 scallion, sliced

1 teaspoon chili oil

1. In a large soup pot, bring the water, carrot, and gingerroot to a boil. Cover and cook over medium heat for 5 minutes.
2. Add the cabbage and continue cooking for another 4 minutes. Bring the soup to a rapid boil and add the soybeans.
3. Lower the heat and stir in the miso paste until it is dissolved.
4. Add the scallion and chili oil to taste and serve hot.

♥ **HEART-HEALTHY TIP:** Soybeans are rich in fiber, which is associated with a lower risk of cardiovascular disease.

NUTRITIONAL INFORMATION PER SERVING

Calories 510

Carbohydrate 37g

Protein 39g

Fat 22g

Fiber 9g

Cholesterol 0mg

Sodium 710mg

African Peanut Stew

⌒ Makes 6 servings

16 ounces firm organic tofu, cubed
2 tablespoons extra-virgin olive oil
1 cup chopped onion
1 cup chopped green bell pepper
1 tablespoon peanut oil or extra-virgin olive oil
4 cloves garlic, minced
2 tablespoons chopped fresh gingerroot
½ cup smooth natural peanut butter
1 14-ounce can plum tomatoes with liquid
1 teaspoon unbleached cane sugar
½ teaspoon cinnamon
½ teaspoon dried thyme
¼ teaspoon allspice
½ teaspoon sea salt
½ teaspoon red pepper flakes
1 cup vegetable stock
2 teaspoons fresh lemon juice
3 cups cooked brown rice
½ cup chopped roasted peanuts

1. Sauté tofu in 2 tablespoons olive oil until tofu becomes crunchy and lightly browned.
2. In a large saucepan, sauté onion and green pepper in oil until onion becomes translucent.
3. Add the garlic and gingerroot and continue cooking for 2 minutes.
4. Stir in the peanut butter, tomatoes, sugar, cinnamon, thyme, allspice, salt, and pepper flakes.
5. Add stock and lemon juice and stir well.
6. Add the sautéed tofu and bring heat up to a boil.

7. Reduce heat to a simmer and continue cooking for 15 minutes.

8. Pour over cooked brown rice in serving bowls and sprinkle top with chopped peanuts.

♥ **HEART-HEALTHY TIP:** Phytosterols such as beta-sitosterol, found in brown rice, decrease cholesterol absorption in the intestine.

NUTRITIONAL INFORMATION PER SERVING

Calories 340

Carbohydrate 37g

Protein 14g

Fat 15g

Fiber 6g

Cholesterol 0mg

Sodium 640mg

Moroccan Chicken and Couscous Stew

⌐ Makes 6 servings

1 cup chopped onion
2 cloves garlic, chopped
1 tablespoon chopped fresh gingerroot
1 jalapeño pepper, seeded and chopped
1 tablespoon extra-virgin olive oil
1 pound boneless and skinless chicken breast, cubed
1 teaspoon curry powder
½ teaspoon ground cumin
½ teaspoon cinnamon
¼ teaspoon cayenne pepper
¼ teaspoon sea salt
¼ teaspoon freshly ground pepper
3 cups sliced mushrooms
1 14-ounce can chopped tomatoes
2 tablespoons peanut butter
1 14-ounce can chicken broth
1 cup couscous
2 cups water
3 tablespoons fresh lemon juice

1. Sauté onion, garlic, gingerroot, and jalapeño in oil in a large saucepan for 10 minutes.
2. Add chicken, curry, cumin, cinnamon, cayenne, salt, and pepper and continue cooking until chicken turns white.
3. Add mushrooms, tomatoes, peanut butter, and chicken broth. Bring to a simmer and cook for an additional 10 minutes.

4. In a separate saucepan, combine the couscous with water and bring to a boil, stirring well. Cover the pan and remove from heat and set aside for 10 minutes to allow couscous to gently finish absorbing the water.

5. Stir the couscous and lemon juice into the chicken stew and serve.

Preparation Tip: The exotic flavor of wild game or fowl is the perfect accompaniment to this stew and can be used in place of the chicken. Or for a vegetarian version of this recipe, simply replace the chicken with tofu.

NUTRITIONAL INFORMATION PER SERVING

Calories 300

Carbohydrate 18g

Protein 30g

Fat 12g

Fiber 2g

Cholesterol 65mg

Sodium 790mg

Chili con Tempeh

⁓ *Makes 6 servings*

3 teaspoons cumin seeds
3 cups chopped onion
1 cup minced tempeh
2 tablespoons extra-virgin olive oil
1 red bell pepper, chopped
1 green bell pepper, chopped
2 tablespoons chopped garlic
1 tablespoon chili powder
1 hot chili pepper, minced
2 teaspoons dried oregano
1 15-ounce can organic black soybeans
1 15-ounce can stewed tomatoes
½ teaspoon sea salt
1 cup chopped cilantro

1. Sauté cumin, onion, tempeh, and oil in a large saucepan over medium heat for 10 minutes.
2. Add bell peppers, garlic, chili powder, chili pepper, and oregano and continue cooking for 5 more minutes.
3. Add soybeans, tomatoes, and salt, and bring to a boil.
4. Cover, reduce heat, and simmer for 30 minutes.
5. Stir in cilantro and serve.

♥ **HEART-HEALTHY TIP:** Soybeans contain phytosterols, which are natural chemicals that resemble cholesterol. Phytosterols compete with dietary cholesterol for absorption by the intestines, resulting in lower blood cholesterol levels.

NUTRITIONAL INFORMATION PER SERVING

Calories 480

Carbohydrate 36g

Protein 35g

Fat 21g

Fiber 10g

Cholesterol 0mg

Sodium 370mg

Spiced Cream of Pumpkin Soup

⁓ Makes 4 servings

1 cup pumpkin seeds
3 large leeks, cleaned and chopped
½ pound carrots, sliced thin
1 tablespoon extra-virgin olive oil
3 cups vegetable broth
1 15-ounce can solid-packed pumpkin
2 cups milk or organic soy milk
¼ teaspoon ground nutmeg
¼ teaspoon ground cinnamon

1. Toast pumpkin seeds in a skillet over high heat, stirring constantly, until they puff up. Remove from heat and set aside.
2. Sauté leeks and carrots in olive oil until browned.
3. Add 2 cups of broth and simmer for about 10 minutes. Pour the leeks, carrots, and broth in a blender and process until creamy. Return to the pan and add the remaining broth, pumpkin, milk, nutmeg, and cinnamon. Cover and simmer for 15 minutes, stirring often, until hot.
4. Pour into serving bowls and sprinkle each bowl with toasted pumpkin seeds.

NUTRITIONAL INFORMATION PER SERVING

Calories 710

Carbohydrate 50g

Protein 24g

Fat 46g

Fiber 5g

Cholesterol 20mg

Sodium 910mg

5

Sauces, Gravies, and Dressings

Sausage Gravy

⌒ Makes 24 servings

4 cups vegetable stock

1 cup water

⅓ cup whole wheat flour

¼ cup extra-virgin olive oil

1 teaspoon low-sodium tamari

1 cup TVP (textured vegetable protein)

Optional Herbs:

½ teaspoon ground sage

½ teaspoon marjoram

¼ teaspoon dried basil

¼ teaspoon dried oregano

¼ teaspoon pepper

1. Boil stock in a saucepan and add your choice of optional herbs.
2. Add flour slowly, stirring constantly with a wire whisk to avoid clumps.
3. Add the oil and tamari and stir well.
4. Add TVP and cook for 5 minutes or until soft.
5. Serve over steamed vegetables, baked potatoes, or biscuits.

NUTRITIONAL INFORMATION PER SERVING

Calories 70

Carbohydrate 5g

Protein 6g

Fat 2.5g

Fiber 1g

Cholesterol 0mg

Sodium 180mg

Peanut Sauce

⁓ *Makes 6 servings*

2 tablespoons peeled and grated fresh gingerroot
1 small chili pepper, seeded and chopped
2 cloves garlic, minced
2 green onions, minced
⅓ cup creamy peanut butter
⅓ cup unsweetened, low-fat coconut milk
3 tablespoons fresh lime juice
2 tablespoons low-sodium tamari
1 teaspoon unbleached cane sugar
¼ cup chopped fresh cilantro

1. Combine gingerroot, chili, garlic, and onions in a mixing bowl.
2. In a separate bowl, whisk together peanut butter, coconut milk, lime juice, tamari, and sugar.
3. Pour the liquids over the vegetables and stir well.
4. Serve peanut sauce over meat, poultry, fish, or rice.
5. Sprinkle top of each serving with cilantro.

Preparation Tip: Buy only unsalted, nonhydrogenated peanut butter.

♥ **HEART-HEALTHY TIP:** Serve over cooked quinoa. Quinoa is a grain rich in saponins, which lower cholesterol and have an antibiotic effect.

NUTRITIONAL INFORMATION PER SERVING

Calories 110	Fiber 1g
Carbohydrate 5g	Cholesterol 0mg
Protein 4g	Sodium 260mg
Fat 8g	

Citus Sauce

Makes 6 servings

Juice of 6 oranges
Juice of 2 lemons
Juice of 2 limes
⅛ teaspoon sea salt
Freshly ground pepper to taste

1. Place all ingredients in a pot over medium heat and simmer until reduced to half.
2. Serve over fish, grains, or legumes.

NUTRITIONAL INFORMATION PER SERVING

Calories 25

Carbohydrate 5g

Protein 0g

Fat 0g

Fiber 0g

Cholesterol 0mg

Sodium 55mg

Sweet Mustard Sauce

Makes 4 servings

½ cup crushed pineapple, canned or fresh
2 tablespoons hot mustard

1. Cook ingredients in a small saucepan over medium heat for approximately 4 minutes.
2. Use as a dipping sauce for chicken, fish, or other seafood.

NUTRITIONAL INFORMATION PER SERVING

Calories 25

Fiber 0g

Carbohydrate 4g

Cholesterol 0mg

Protein 0g

Sodium 55mg

Fat 1g

Roasted Red Pepper Sauce

⁓ Makes 4 servings

6 large red bell peppers
3 heads garlic (about 30 cloves)
1 cup crushed tomatoes, fresh or canned
1 tablespoon balsamic vinegar
¼ teaspoon sea salt
⅛ teaspoon cayenne pepper

1. Place the bell peppers on baking sheet. Turning occasionally, broil until they become charred black. Place them in a brown paper bag for 2 minutes. Remove the peppers, peel the charred skin off, and remove the tops and seeds.
2. Bake the garlic at 350°F for 1 hour, or until the cloves are soft. Squeeze the garlic from the paper cloves and place in a blender. Add the tomatoes and bell peppers and blend until well mixed.
3. Add the balsamic vinegar, salt, pepper, and cayenne and blend again.
4. Pour over pasta, fish, grilled eggplant, or steamed vegetables.

NUTRITIONAL INFORMATION PER SERVING

Calories 110

Carbohydrate 21g

Protein 5g

Fat 0g

Fiber 6g

Cholesterol 0mg

Sodium 300mg

Yogurt Sauce

Makes 6 servings

1 pint plain nonfat yogurt
2 tablespoons dried dill
2 tablespoons dried parsley
2 tablespoons fresh lemon juice
½ teaspoon cracked pepper
2 cloves garlic, chopped

1. Combine all ingredients.
2. Serve over fish or spicy meat dishes.

NUTRITIONAL INFORMATION PER SERVING

Calories 45

Carbohydrate 7g

Protein 4g

Fat 0g

Fiber 0g

Cholesterol 0mg

Sodium 55mg

Creamy Garlic Dressing

~ Makes 4 servings

1 scallion, chopped
4 cloves garlic
2 teaspoons fresh lemon juice
1 tablespoon balsamic vinegar
½ teaspoon unbleached cane sugar
1 10–14 ounce package silken organic tofu
1 teaspoon dried oregano
1 tablespoon flaxseed oil
Freshly ground black pepper to taste

1. In a blender or food processor, combine scallion, garlic, lemon juice, vinegar, and sugar. Process until ingredients are well mixed and finely chopped.
2. Use a spatula to scrape down the sides and add tofu, oregano, and oil. Blend until creamy.
3. Add black pepper to taste.
4. Serve over salad, cooked vegetables, baked potatoes, or pasta or use in place of mayonnaise in a sandwich.

♥ **HEART-HEALTHY TIP:** A lack of essential fatty acids (EFAS) in the diet plays a significant role in the development of chronic degenerative diseases such as heart disease, multiple sclerosis, cancer, and rheumatoid arthritis. Experts estimate that 80 percent of the American population does not get enough EFAS. EFAS are found in fish oil and flaxseed oil.

NUTRITIONAL INFORMATION PER SERVING

Calories 100	Fiber 1g
Carbohydrate 4g	Cholesterol 0mg
Protein 7g	Sodium 35mg
Fat 6g	

Yogurt Curry Sauce

Makes 4 servings

1 cup plain nonfat yogurt
2 teaspoons curry powder
1 teaspoon fresh lemon juice

1. Stir all ingredients together.
2. Use as a dip or as a flavoring for fish, steamed vegetables, rice, or pasta.

NUTRITIONAL INFORMATION PER SERVING

Calories 35

Carbohydrate 5g

Protein 3g

Fat 0g

Fiber 0g

Cholesterol 0mg

Sodium 45mg

Asian Dressing

⁓ Makes 8 servings

½ lemon, peeled
1 2-inch piece fresh gingerroot, peeled
2 tablespoons low-sodium tamari
2 tablespoons balsamic vinegar
5 cloves garlic
2 tablespoons flaxseed oil or extra-virgin olive oil

1. Peel the lemon by cutting off just the very bright yellow outside part of the peel, leaving the inner white pithy part, which contains all the fruit's beneficial bioflavonoids.
2. Combine all ingredients in a blender and blend for 30 seconds to 1 minute. If you prefer a creamier dressing simply blend longer. To thin the dressing, add a tablespoon of water and blend again.

3. Serve over leafy greens, steamed vegetables, fish, beans, lentils, rice, or cooked grains.

♥ **HEART-HEALTHY TIP:** Lemons contain bioflavonoids, vitamin C, and potassium. These antioxidants and their natural anticarcinogens help prevent infections, cancer, heart disease, stroke, and high blood pressure.

NUTRITIONAL INFORMATION PER SERVING

Calories 40
Carbohydrate 2g
Protein 0g
Fat 3.5g

Fiber 0g
Cholesterol 0mg
Sodium 0mg

Tamari Mustard Marinade

⌒ Makes 4 servings

2 tablespoons fresh lime juice
¼ cup flaxseed or extra-virgin olive oil
2 tablespoons low-sodium tamari
2 tablespoons balsamic vinegar
2 teaspoons brown mustard

1. In a large bowl, mix all ingredients well.
2. Use as a marinade for fish, meat, poultry, or polenta slices.

NUTRITIONAL INFORMATION PER SERVING

Calories 140

Carbohydrate 2g

Protein 1g

Fat 14g

Fiber 0g

Cholesterol 0mg

Sodium 320mg

Pecan Cranberry Sauce

⁓ Makes 4 servings

1 cup cranberries

½ cup chopped pecans

1 orange, peeled and chopped

1 teaspoon orange zest

1 tablespoon minced fresh gingerroot

2 tablespoons maple syrup

2 tablespoons unrefined cane sugar

1. Cook all ingredients in a saucepan over medium heat for 15 minutes.
2. Chill and serve.

♥ **HEART-HEALTHY TIP:** Warming spices, such as ginger and cayenne, create heat and bring blood to the capillaries surrounding the stomach, thus aiding in digestion.

NUTRITIONAL INFORMATION PER SERVING

Calories 190

Carbohydrate 25g

Protein 1g

Fat 10g

Fiber 2g

Cholesterol 0mg

Sodium 0mg

6

Fish, Seafood, and Sea Vegetables

Spicy Salsa and Fish

Makes 6 servings

FISH

1 tablespoon toasted sesame oil
1 teaspoon mild paprika
1 teaspoon crushed dried thyme
¼ teaspoon sea salt
1 clove garlic, pressed
6 6-ounce fillets flaky white fish

SALSA

4 large ripe tomatoes, chopped
¼ cup red onion, chopped
1 cup cilantro, chopped
3 cloves garlic, chopped
¼ jalapeño pepper, chopped
1 teaspoon fresh oregano, chopped *or* a pinch of crushed dried oregano
¼ teaspoon freshly ground sea salt
Pinch of freshly ground black pepper

Directions for Fish

1. With a mortar and pestle, grind together the oil, paprika, thyme, salt, and garlic until a smooth paste forms.
2. Rub the paste over the fish fillets.
3. Broil the fish in oven for about 7 minutes. (The cooking time will vary depending on the thickness of the fish fillets.)

Directions for Salsa

1. Combine the salsa ingredients in a large bowl and mix together thoroughly. Set aside.
2. When the fish is cooked thoroughly, scoop ¼ cup salsa over each fish fillet and serve immediately.

♥ **HEART-HEALTHY TIP:** People who eat fish regularly are at lower risk of a fatal heart attack than those who avoid fish totally. In a thirty-year study of 1,822 men, those who reported eating two servings a week were almost half as likely to die from a heart attack than those who did not eat any fish.

NUTRITIONAL INFORMATION PER SERVING

Calories 210

Carbohydrate 0g

Protein 41g

Fat 5g

Fiber 0g

Cholesterol 115mg

Sodium 280mg

Shrimp Cocktail

⌇ Makes 4 servings

1 pound medium shrimp, shelled and deveined
½ cup chili sauce
2 tablespoons finely chopped cilantro
1 tablespoon lime juice
3 teaspoons prepared white horseradish
½ teaspoon ground cumin
1 lime, quartered

1. In a saucepan, boil enough water to cover shrimp.
2. Add shrimp and reduce heat to medium and cook until shrimp become opaque, about 2 minutes.
3. Drain, rinse with cold water, and cover and refrigerate for 30 minutes.
4. In a small bowl, mix chili sauce, cilantro, lime juice, horseradish, and cumin.
5. Cover the sauce and chill, about 30 minutes.
6. Divide the shrimp on four plates; serve with sauce and lime wedges.

NUTRITIONAL INFORMATION PER SERVING

Calories 140
Carbohydrate 8g
Protein 25g
Fat 1.5g

Fiber 2g
Cholesterol 220mg
Sodium 660mg

Sweet Onion and Arame Sauté

⌐ *Makes 4 servings*

¼ cup dried arame

2 sweet onions, sliced

1 tablespoon sesame oil

2 tablespoons water

3 tablespoons low-sodium tamari

2 tablespoons sesame seeds, roasted

1. Soak arame for 5 minutes, rinse and drain.
2. Sauté onions in sesame oil for 2 to 3 minutes.
3. Add arame and water. Cover and bring to a simmer, then turn heat to low.
4. Add tamari, cover, and simmer for 40 to 50 minutes.
5. Add more tamari if desired and sprinkle with sesame seeds.
6. Serve warm or cold.

♥ **HEART-HEALTHY TIP:** A recent study from the University of Chile found that algae, including arame, can be an excellent dietary fiber source and are very useful in the prevention or treatment of fiber-deficiency-related diseases.

NUTRITIONAL INFORMATION PER SERVING

Calories 160	Fiber 8g
Carbohydrate 15g	Cholesterol 0mg
Protein 9g	Sodium 490mg
Fat 7g	

Hijiki Salad

⌁ Makes 4 servings

1 cup soaked, drained, and chopped hijiki

¼ yellow onion, chopped

5 mushrooms, chopped

2 tablespoons sesame oil

2 tablespoons rice vinegar

1 tablespoon fresh lemon juice

1 carrot, grated

1 tablespoon low-sodium tamari

2–4 cups chopped greens (spinach, romaine, or steamed kale)

1. Sauté hijiki, onion, and mushrooms in oil 20 to 30 minutes.
2. Add vinegar, lemon, carrot, and tamari.
3. Allow to cool.
4. Serve over chopped greens.

♥ **HEART-HEALTHY TIP:** Sea vegetables such as hijiki are a significant source of omega-3 fatty acids.

NUTRITIONAL INFORMATION PER SERVING

Calories 130

Carbohydrate 12g

Protein 4g

Fat 7g

Fiber 6g

Cholesterol 0mg

Sodium 280mg

Kombu Chips

~ *Makes 2 servings*

Several long pieces of kombu (about 1 ounce dry weight)
¼ cup extra-virgin olive oil

1. Soak kombu in water for 10 minutes until soft.
2. Heat olive oil in a small frying pan over medium heat.
3. With scissors, cut the kombu into long strips about ⅛ inch wide and 3 inches long. Tie into knots.
4. Deep-fry in oil until crispy, about 5 minutes. Set on paper towels to dry. Discard the used oil in pan.
5. Serve as a snack just as you would serve potato chips. These crunchy treats have the texture of potato chips and are a nutritious snack any time of day.

♥ **HEART-HEALTHY TIP:** Sea vegetables such as kombu are a good vegetarian source of bioavailable vitamin B_{12}.

NUTRITIONAL INFORMATION PER SERVING

Calories 35

Carbohydrate 1g

Protein 0g

Fat 3.5g

Fiber 0g

Cholesterol 0mg

Sodium 15mg

Toasted Nori Squares

Makes 4 servings

4 sheets nori
2 tablespoons freshly grated gingerroot
2 tablespoons low-sodium tamari
2 tablespoons mirin

1. Toast the nori by holding each sheet at the edge and passing it horizontally about 5 inches above a stove flame or element.
2. When the nori becomes dry and crisp, cut the sheets into 2-inch squares and place several squares of nori on a serving plate.
3. Place a pinch of grated gingerroot and 2 to 3 drops of tamari and mirin on each.
4. Fold up the nori with the gingerroot and sauce inside. Serve immediately.

Preparation Tip: Be mindful not to burn your fingers when toasting the sheets of nori. This process mellows the ocean flavor and gives the nori a crisper texture.

NUTRITIONAL INFORMATION PER SERVING

Calories 35
Carbohydrate 6g
Protein 2g
Fat 0g

Fiber 1g
Cholesterol 0mg
Sodium 310mg

Fish and Eggplant Curry

~ *Makes 4 servings*

1 ½ teaspoons extra-virgin olive oil

3 cups chopped eggplant

1 cup chopped yellow onion

2 cups sliced mushrooms

2 tablespoons red curry paste

1 cup reduced-fat coconut milk

1 pound fish (such as cod, halibut, or trout)

1 cup cooked brown rice

1. Heat the olive oil in a large skillet over medium heat. Add the eggplant, onion, and mushrooms and cook for 5 minutes, stirring occasionally. Stir in the curry paste and coconut milk.
2. Place the fish in the skillet on top of the curry sauce and cook for another 10 minutes, turning the fish as needed until it is thoroughly cooked.
3. Break up the fish and mix it into the sauce.
4. Place the rice onto serving plates and pour curry sauce over rice.

♥ **HEART-HEALTHY TIP:** Fish oil in the diet helps lower blood pressure by stimulating nitric oxide vasodilation.

NUTRITIONAL INFORMATION PER SERVING

Calories 300	Fiber 4g
Carbohydrate 20g	Cholesterol 75mg
Protein 30g	Sodium 125mg
Fat 11g	

Roasted Salmon

◦── *Makes 10 servings*

¼ cup chopped fresh dill
1 cup finely diced shallots
2 tablespoons fresh thyme
3 tablespoons fresh rosemary
½ cup dry vermouth
4 pounds salmon, filleted and scaled
¼ teaspoon sea salt
½ teaspoon freshly ground pepper
3 tablespoons extra-virgin olive oil

1. In the bottom of a roasting pan, place dill, shallots, thyme, rosemary, and vermouth.
2. Place salmon on top of herbs in roasting pan. Sprinkle with salt and pepper, and rub with olive oil.
3. Roast under broiler, 6 inches from the heat until the skin is crisp about 12 to 15 minutes.
4. Remove from heat, slice into strips, and serve with Citrus Sauce (See Index).

♥ **HEART-HEALTHY TIP:** The carotenoids are a huge family of more than 600 yellow to red antioxidant pigments of which beta-carotene is the most famous. Beta-carotene and alpha-carotene put the orange into carrots, lycopene puts the red into tomatoes and watermelon, and astaxanthin puts the pink into lobsters and salmon.

NUTRITIONAL INFORMATION PER SERVING

Calories 360	Fiber 0g
Carbohydrate 0g	Cholesterol 105mg
Protein 50g	Sodium 150mg
Fat 18g	

7

Vegetables

Chard with Garlic Sauce

....

~⌐ *Makes 6 servings*

½ pound fresh chard
1 ½ cups organic soy milk
1 tablespoon butter
½ teaspoon dried dill
½ teaspoon dried thyme
½ teaspoon dried basil
2 teaspoons garlic powder
½ teaspoon sea salt
½ teaspoon black pepper
3 teaspoons whole wheat flour
6 tablespoons nutritional yeast

1. Steam chard in a saucepan for 5 to 8 minutes, until soft.
2. In a small saucepan, combine remaining ingredients except the nutritional yeast and heat slowly, stirring constantly until mixture begins to thicken.
3. Add the nutritional yeast and mix well.
4. Pour sauce over chard and serve immediately. The garlic sauce is delicious as gravy over root vegetables, fish, beans, and grains.

♥ **HEART-HEALTHY TIP:** Nutritional yeast is a rich source of the minerals necessary for cardiovascular health such as calcium, potassium, iron, magnesium, and zinc. Garlic is a natural antibiotic that will help stave off bacterial and viral infections, and it contains numerous anticancer compounds.

NUTRITIONAL INFORMATION PER SERVING

Calories 130	Fiber 8g
Carbohydrate 15g	Cholesterol 5mg
Protein 11g	Sodium 230mg
Fat 3g	

Mashed Potato and Jerusalem Artichokes

⌐ Makes 4 servings

4 medium russet potatoes
1 Jerusalem artichoke, chopped
½ cup organic soy milk

1. Boil potatoes and artichoke in water until soft.
2. Drain and place in a blender or food processor with soy milk. Process until smooth, adding more soy milk to obtain desired consistency.

Preparation Tip: The Jerusalem artichoke adds a creamy rich texture so butter is not necessary.

NUTRITIONAL INFORMATION PER SERVING

Calories 140

Carbohydrate 30g

Protein 3g

Fat 0.5g

Fiber 2g

Cholesterol 0mg

Sodium 410mg

Ginger Glazed Carrots

∽ *Makes 4 servings*

2 pounds carrots, peeled, cut lengthwise into thirds and
then into 2-inch pieces

1 teaspoon finely julienned orange zest

1 ½ cups fresh orange juice

2 cloves garlic, minced

⅓ cup thinly sliced scallion whites

2 teaspoons unbleached cane sugar

2 tablespoons organic butter

2 teaspoons grated fresh gingerroot

½ teaspoon sea salt

¼ cup thinly sliced scallion greens

1. In a large saucepan, combine carrots, orange zest,
   orange juice, garlic, scallion whites, sugar, butter,
   gingerroot, and salt. Bring to a boil over medium heat,
   stirring occasionally.
2. Cover and continue cooking for an additional 5
   minutes.
3. Stir in scallion greens and spoon into serving bowls.

NUTRITIONAL INFORMATION PER SERVING

Calories 220

Carbohydrate 36g

Protein 3g

Fat 7g

Fiber 7g

Cholesterol 15mg

Sodium 430mg

Peas and Pearl Onions

Makes 6 servings

10 ounces fresh, peeled pearl onions *or* 1 10-ounce
    package frozen pearl onions

2 tablespoons extra-virgin olive oil

1 teaspoon unbleached cane sugar

2 tablespoons balsamic vinegar

⅔ cup water

4 cloves garlic, minced

1½ cups chopped scallions

2 10-ounce packages frozen peas

½ teaspoon sea salt

1 teaspoon organic butter

1. In a skillet, sauté onions in oil for about 1 minute.

2. Sprinkle the sugar over the onions, stirring
   occasionally, and allow them to brown.

3. Add vinegar and water and bring to a boil. Simmer for
   about 15 minutes.

4. Stir in the garlic and scallions and continue cooking for
   about 2 minutes.

5. Stir in peas and salt, cover, and continue to cook until
   peas are heated through, about 5 minutes.

6. Stir in butter and heat until butter is melted.

7. Stir and serve.

NUTRITIONAL INFORMATION PER SERVING

Calories 130

Carbohydrate 16g

Protein 5g

Fat 6g

Fiber 4g

Cholesterol 0mg

Sodium 370mg

Zesty Garlic Peppers

~ *Makes 4 servings*

2 red bell peppers, chopped

2 green bell peppers, chopped

2 yellow bell peppers, chopped

1 teaspoon extra-virgin olive oil

4 cloves garlic, minced

1 teaspoon orange zest

1 tablespoon tomato paste

½ teaspoon sea salt

1 teaspoon dried oregano

¼ teaspoon freshly ground black pepper

1. Sauté peppers in olive oil, stirring frequently for about 5 minutes.
2. Add garlic and continue cooking for another minute.
3. Add orange zest, tomato paste, salt, oregano, and black pepper.
4. Continue cooking for 3 minutes and serve.

NUTRITIONAL INFORMATION PER SERVING

Calories 60

Carbohydrate 10g

Protein 3g

Fat 1.5g

Fiber 4g

Cholesterol 0mg

Sodium 310mg

Baked Root Vegetable Fries

~ Makes 4 servings

1 large russet potato
1 rutabaga
1 carrot
1 beet
1 tablespoon extra-virgin olive oil
¼ teaspoon crushed dried rosemary
¼ teaspoon crushed dried basil
½ teaspoon mild paprika
½ teaspoon sea salt

1. Preheat oven to 450°F.
2. Slice the root vegetables into long thin strips.
3. Combine all ingredients in a large bowl. Toss until vegetables are well coated with oil and seasonings.
4. Spread onto a baking sheet and bake for 15 minutes. Remove from oven and turn vegetables over. Continue baking for another 15 minutes, or until golden brown.

NUTRITIONAL INFORMATION PER SERVING

Calories 90

Carbohydrate 12g

Protein 2g

Fat 3.5g

Fiber 4g

Cholesterol 0mg

Sodium 370mg

Miso Pesto and Potatoes

⌒ Makes 8 servings

3 cups chopped potato

3 cups chopped onion

2 cups spinach

1 cup Italian parsley or cilantro

1 cup chopped walnuts

1 tablespoon mild white miso

2–4 cloves garlic

¼ cup extra-virgin olive oil

¼ cup water

1. In a large covered saucepan or pressure cooker, cook potatoes and onions in water for 10 to 15 minutes.
2. To make the pesto, blend together in a blender or food professor the spinach, parsley, walnuts, miso, garlic, olive oil, and water, using a spatula to scrape the sides when necessary. Add a few tablespoons of water if necessary.
3. Toss the potatoes and onion in the pesto and serve hot.

Preparation Tip: This dish can be stored in a covered container in the refrigerator for up to three days and can be served cold as the exotic cousin to potato salad. Other root vegetables can also be used in place of, or in addition to, the potatoes.

NUTRITIONAL INFORMATION PER SERVING

Calories 260

Carbohydrate 26g

Protein 7g

Fat 14g

Fiber 4g

Cholesterol 0mg

Sodium 100mg

Green Beans with Almonds

∽ Makes 4 servings

2 cups fresh green beans
¼ cup slivered almonds
2 tablespoons low-sodium tamari
3 tablespoons water

1. Place all ingredients in a skillet, cover, and cook over medium heat for 5 minutes or until beans are soft.

♥ **HEART-HEALTHY TIP:** Almonds are a rich source of magnesium, containing 86 mg in each ounce.

NUTRITIONAL INFORMATION PER SERVING

Calories 90

Carbohydrate 7g

Protein 4g

Fat 4.5g

Fiber 3g

Cholesterol 0mg

Sodium 310mg

8

Desserts

Kahlúa and Cream Pudding

~ *Makes 4 servings*

10 ounces organic silken tofu
¼ cup sweetened cocoa powder
2 tablespoons Kahlúa
2 teaspoons vanilla extract

1. Blend all ingredients in a food processor or blender, using a spatula to scrape down the sides.
2. Pour into serving dishes and chill for 5 to 10 minutes before serving.

♥ **HEART-HEALTHY TIP:** Tofu is a rich source of magnesium containing 118 mg per half cup.

NUTRITIONAL INFORMATION PER SERVING

Calories 130

Carbohydrate 12g

Protein 7g

Fat 5g

Fiber 1g

Cholesterol 0mg

Sodium 40mg

Chocolate Tofu Pudding

Makes 4 servings

1 pound organic silken tofu
1 cup chocolate chips

1. In a blender or food processor, blend the tofu until it is smooth. Add a few tablespoons of water if necessary.
2. In a small saucepan or double boiler, melt the chocolate chips, stirring frequently. As soon as the chips melt, pour them into the blender with the tofu.
3. Blend until smooth, scraping the sides of the blender with a spatula to mix all of the tofu into the chocolate.
4. Pour into dessert cups or pie shell and chill for at least 30 minutes to set.

♥ **HEART-HEALTHY TIP:** Soy food contains about 34 percent protein and is also a substantial source of several minerals, including calcium, iron, copper, zinc, phosphorus, potassium, and magnesium.

NUTRITIONAL INFORMATION PER SERVING

Calories 370

Carbohydrate 39g

Protein 13g

Fat 18g

Fiber 3g

Cholesterol 10mg

Sodium 160mg

Apple Cobbler

⌒ Makes 8 servings

PIE DOUGH

1 cup whole wheat flour

3 tablespoons unbleached cane sugar

1 teaspoon grated lemon zest

¼ teaspoon sea salt

¼ teaspoon baking powder

3 tablespoons organic butter

¼ cup organic sour cream

FILLING

6 Granny Smith apples, peeled, cored, and sliced thin

¾ cup unbleached cane sugar

1 tablespoon whole wheat flour

2 teaspoons fresh lemon juice

1 teaspoon cinnamon

¼ teaspoon freshly ground nutmeg

⅛ teaspoon sea salt

2 teaspoons organic butter

Directions for Pie Dough

1. Combine flour, sugar, lemon zest, salt, and baking powder in a bowl.
2. Shred butter with a cheese grater into flour.
3. Stir in sour cream and slowly add 2 tablespoons cold water until dough comes together. Make into 2 balls and refrigerate for 30 minutes.

Filling

1. Preheat oven to 425°F.
2. In a large bowl, combine apples, sugar, and flour.
3. Add lemon juice, cinnamon, nutmeg, and salt.

4. On a lightly floured board, pat out the chilled dough into two 8-inch disks. Line a pie dish with 1 of the disks.

5. Spoon the spiced apples into the pie dish and drop pieces of the remaining 2 teaspoons of butter over the top. Place the remaining dough on top of the apple filling.

6. Bake for 15 minutes.

7. Reduce oven heat to 350°F and bake for another 25 minutes.

8. Transfer to a wire rack and cool for 10 minutes. Serve warm.

NUTRITIONAL INFORMATION PER SERVING

Calories 280

Carbohydrate 50g

Protein 3g

Fat 7g

Fiber 4g

Cholesterol 20mg

Sodium 180mg

Ginger Cookies

⁓ *Makes 24 cookies*

1 ½ cups whole wheat flour
½ cup raisins
½ cup finely chopped walnuts
½ cup chopped dates
½ cup butter
1 cup honey
1 egg
1 cup silken organic tofu
2 tablespoons freshly grated gingerroot
2 tablespoons ginger powder
2 tablespoons cinnamon
2 teaspoons nutmeg
½ teaspoon sea salt
1 tablespoon vanilla extract

1. Preheat oven to 400°F.
2. In a large bowl, combine whole wheat flour, raisins, walnuts, and dates.
3. In a blender or food processor, combine butter, honey, egg, tofu, gingerroot, ginger powder, cinnamon, nutmeg, salt, and vanilla.
4. Pour the blended ingredients into the bowl with the flour mixture and stir well.
5. Drop by teaspoonfuls onto a nonstick or lightly oiled baking sheet and bake at 400°F for 10 to 15 minutes.

NUTRITIONAL INFORMATION PER COOKIE

Calories 170
Carbohydrate 24g
Protein 3g
Fat 6g

Fiber 1g
Cholesterol 15mg
Sodium 90mg

9

Smoothies and Cold Drinks

Vanilla Shake

⌣ Makes 1 serving

1 frozen banana
½ cup plain nonfat yogurt
½ cup silken organic tofu
1 tablespoon flaxmeal (ground flaxseeds)
1 teaspoon vanilla extract

1. Freeze the banana ahead of time by peeling it and placing it into a plastic bag in the freezer. Do not freeze with the peel intact; it is very difficult to remove once frozen.
2. Combine all ingredients in a blender, and blend until smooth and creamy.
3. Drink immediately.

Preparation Tip: Flaxseed that is preground can be purchased in packages, but it will become rancid much more quickly than whole flaxseeds. Therefore, it is best to buy whole flaxseeds and store them in the refrigerator to keep them fresh. When ready to use, pour the measured amount into a coffee grinder or food processor and grind into a meal.

♥ **HEART-HEALTHY TIP:** Ground flaxseed contains linolenic acid, which protects against heart attacks and abnormal rhythms.

NUTRITIONAL INFORMATION PER SERVING

Calories 300
Carbohydrate 43g
Protein 17g
Fat 7g

Fiber 6g
Cholesterol 0mg
Sodium 190mg

Berry Vanilla Smoothie

~ *Makes 2 servings*

1 cup organic vanilla soy milk
6 ounces plain nonfat yogurt
½ cup frozen strawberries
½ cup silken organic tofu
1 teaspoon vanilla extract

1. Place all ingredients in a blender and process until smooth.
2. Drink immediately.

♥ **HEART-HEALTHY TIP:** Studies have found that when soy protein is substituted for animal protein in the diet, levels of total cholesterol, LDL cholesterol, and triglycerides are decreased without lowering the healthy HDL cholesterol. The average soy protein intake in these studies was 47 grams per day but beneficial effects were seen at intakes as low as 30 grams per day. You can get this amount of soy protein by drinking two cups of soy milk or eating 112 grams of tofu.

NUTRITIONAL INFORMATION PER SERVING

Calories 180

Carbohydrate 23g

Protein 13g

Fat 4.5g

Fiber 2g

Cholesterol 0mg

Sodium 140mg

Peaches and Cream Smoothie

Makes 2 servings

1 frozen banana
1 cup organic vanilla soy milk
1 cup sliced peaches, fresh or canned
2 tablespoons unbleached cane sugar
1 teaspoon vanilla extract

1. Freeze the banana ahead of time by peeling it and placing it into a plastic bag in the freezer. Do not freeze with the peel intact; it is very difficult to remove once frozen.
2. Combine all ingredients in a blender and blend until smooth and creamy.
3. Drink immediately.

NUTRITIONAL INFORMATION PER SERVING

Calories 240

Carbohydrate 49g

Protein 4g

Fat 3g

Fiber 4g

Cholesterol 0mg

Sodium 60mg

Creamy Orange Smoothie

~ Makes 1 serving

1 frozen banana
1 cup plain nonfat yogurt
2 tablespoons frozen orange juice concentrate
1 tablespoon flaxseed oil
1 tablespoon oat bran

1. Freeze the banana ahead of time by peeling it and placing it into a plastic bag in the freezer. Do not freeze with the peel intact; it is very difficult to remove once frozen.
2. Place all ingredients into a blender. Process until smooth.
3. Drink immediately.

NUTRITIONAL INFORMATION PER SERVING

Calories 370

Carbohydrate 55g

Protein 16g

Fat 10g

Fiber 4g

Cholesterol 5mg

Sodium 180mg

Tropical Sunrise Smoothie

~ *Makes 2 servings*

1 frozen banana
1 cup organic soy milk
½ cup chopped mango
½ cup crushed pineapple, fresh or canned

1. Freeze the banana ahead of time by peeling it and placing it into a plastic bag in the freezer. Do not freeze with the peel intact; it is very difficult to remove once frozen.
2. Combine all ingredients in a blender. Process until smooth.
3. Drink immediately.

NUTRITIONAL INFORMATION PER SERVING

Calories 180

Carbohydrate 33g

Protein 5g

Fat 3g

Fiber 3g

Cholesterol 0mg

Sodium 20mg

Soy Nog Smoothie

Makes 1 serving

1 frozen banana
1 cup organic vanilla soy milk
¼ teaspoon nutmeg

1. Freeze the banana ahead of time by peeling it and placing it into a plastic bag in the freezer. Do not freeze with the peel intact; it is very difficult to remove once frozen.
2. Combine all ingredients in a blender. Process until smooth.
3. Drink immediately.

NUTRITIONAL INFORMATION PER SERVING

Calories 270

Carbohydrate 47g

Protein 7g

Fat 6g

Fiber 3g

Cholesterol 0mg

Sodium 120mg

Piña Colada Smoothie

....

⌣ Makes 1 serving

1 cup organic plain soy milk
½ cup crushed pineapple, fresh or canned
1 teaspoon coconut extract

1. Combine all ingredients in a blender. Process until smooth.
2. Drink immediately.

NUTRITIONAL INFORMATION PER SERVING

Calories 180

Carbohydrate 27g

Protein 6g

Fat 5g

Fiber 1g

Cholesterol 0mg

Sodium 140mg

Tropical Fruit Punch

~ Makes 2 servings

½ cup pineapple juice
½ cup orange juice
1 tablespoon fresh lemon juice
1 ripe banana
½ cup sparkling water

1. Pour all fruit juices in a blender, add the banana, and puree until smooth.
2. Pour into glass. Add sparkling water and stir.
3. Serve immediately.

NUTRITIONAL INFORMATION PER SERVING

Calories 120

Carbohydrate 27g

Protein 1g

Fat 0g

Fiber 2g

Cholesterol 0mg

Sodium 0mg

Lemon Lime Punch

⌣ Makes 1 serving

½ cup unsweetened apple juice
½ cup sparkling water
1 tablespoon fresh lime juice
1 tablespoon fresh lemon juice

1. Stir ingredients together and serve over ice. If desired, add a fresh mint leaf and/or a lemon or lime wedge.

NUTRITIONAL INFORMATION PER SERVING

Calories 70

Carbohydrate 16g

Protein 0g

Fat 0g

Fiber 0g

Cholesterol 0mg

Sodium 0mg

Orange Smoothie

~ *Makes 1 serving*

1 frozen banana
1 orange, peeled
¼ cup plain nonfat yogurt
1 tablespoon frozen orange juice concentrate

1. Freeze the banana ahead of time by peeling it and placing it into a plastic bag in the freezer. Do not freeze with the peel intact; it is very difficult to remove once frozen.
2. Use a knife to cut away just the outside bright orange part of the orange peel, leaving the white pithy part, which contains all of the fruit's beneficial bioflavonoids.
3. Blend all ingredients together in a blender until smooth and creamy.
4. Drink immediately.

♥ **HEART-HEALTHY TIP:** Oranges contain the antioxidant vitamin C, which may help to prevent the formation of thrombi. In a double-blind study surgical patients were given 1 gram of vitamin C each day. They developed significantly fewer life-threatening thrombi than those who did not receive the vitamin C.

NUTRITIONAL INFORMATION PER SERVING

Calories 220	Fiber 6g
Carbohydrate 48g	Cholesterol 0mg
Protein 6g	Sodium 45mg
Fat 0.5g	

10

Hot Drinks

Cinnamon Nightcap

⌇ Makes 1 serving

1 cup organic soy milk
1 teaspoon honey
1 cinnamon herb tea bag

1. In a small saucepan, combine the ingredients. Warm over low heat, stirring occasionally.
2. Remove tea bag and pour into a mug.

NUTRITIONAL INFORMATION PER SERVING

Calories 130

Carbohydrate 24g

Protein 4g

Fat 2g

Fiber 1g

Cholesterol 0mg

Sodium 100mg

Carob Mint Nip

....

Makes 1 serving

1 cup organic soy milk
1 peppermint herb tea bag
1 teaspoon carob powder
1 teaspoon honey or maple syrup

1. In a small saucepan, heat milk with tea bag over low heat.
2. Combine carob powder and honey in a cup and stir well.
3. Remove tea bag from saucepan and discard.
4. Pour herbed milk into cup, stir and serve.

NUTRITIONAL INFORMATION PER SERVING

....

Calories 160

Carbohydrate 22g

Protein 7g

Fat 5g

Fiber 0g

Cholesterol 0mg

Sodium 115mg

Green Tea

~ Makes 1 serving

1 caffeine-free green tea bag
1 cup boiling water

1. Steep the tea bag in hot water for about 5 minutes.
2. Drink immediately.

♥ **Heart-Healthy Tip:** The black and green tea polyphenols should be included in a healthy diet because studies show they have many health benefits; they may reduce cholesterol absorption in the intestine, decrease blood coagulation, decrease blood pressure, and inhibit the growth of vascular smooth muscle cells.

NUTRITIONAL INFORMATION PER SERVING

Calories 0

Fiber 0g

Carbohydrate 0g

Cholesterol 0mg

Protein 0g

Sodium 5mg

Fat 0g

Soy Milk Latte

....

~ *Makes 1 serving*

1 cup organic vanilla soy milk
1–2 tablespoons unbleached cane sugar
1–2 teaspoons grain beverage crystals

1. Heat all ingredients in a small saucepan just until hot.
2. Serve immediately.

Preparation Tip: Grain beverages are caffeine-free coffee substitutes such as Inka, Caffix, and Postum. There are numerous grain-beverage products on the market, each with its own flavor.

NUTRITIONAL INFORMATION PER SERVING
....

Calories 210

Carbohydrate 36g

Protein 6g

Fat 5g

Fiber 0g

Cholesterol 0mg

Sodium 120mg

Soy Nog

~ *Makes 1 serving*

1 cup organic vanilla soy milk
1 tablespoon unbleached cane sugar
½ teaspoon vanilla extract
¼ teaspoon rum extract
Pinch of nutmeg

1. Combine all ingredients except nutmeg in a blender and blend until smooth.
2. Heat in a small saucepan over medium-high heat for 5 minutes.
3. Pour into a mug and sprinkle with nutmeg.
4. Serve immediately.

NUTRITIONAL INFORMATION PER SERVING

Calories 200

Carbohydrate 31g

Protein 7g

Fat 5g

Fiber 0g

Cholesterol 0mg

Sodium 115mg

Soy Milk Cocoa

....

~⁀ *Makes 1 serving*

1 cup organic vanilla soy milk
1 tablespoon cocoa powder
2 tablespoons unbleached cane sugar

1. Combine all ingredients in a blender and blend until smooth and frothy.
2. Heat in small saucepan over medium-high heat for 5 minutes.
3. Serve hot.

NUTRITIONAL INFORMATION PER SERVING

Calories 290

Carbohydrate 49g

Protein 7g

Fat 7g

Fiber 0g

Cholesterol 0mg

Sodium 130mg

Glossary

Antioxidants: Antioxidants are literally substances that prevent oxidation, or the removal of electrons from molecules, to free radicals, thereby preventing cellular damage. Common natural antioxidants include vitamins C and E and beta-carotene. Antioxidants neutralize free radicals (the damaging molecules), which are created in our bodies from a variety of situations such as aging, chemical or radiation exposure, stress, and disease. When antioxidant nutrients bind with free radicals they become neutral and stop wreaking havoc on the immune system. There are many antioxidant sources such as fresh fruits, vegetables, and supplements such as grape seed and pine bark.

Barley Malt Syrup: Sprouted barley liquid is dark brown in color, thick and sticky like molasses, and has a rich malt flavor. Buy only 100 percent barley products. Many inferior products contain corn malt syrup, which dilutes flavor and adds unnecessary simplified sugars. Buy only organic barley malt syrup. Store in the refrigerator and heat jar under hot water to help liquefy when ready to use.

Brown Rice Syrup: Brown rice syrup is less refined than table sugar and contains many of the nutrients contained in brown rice. Brown rice syrup has an amber color and a mild butterscotch flavor. It is not as sweet as white sugar and can be mixed with other sweeteners. Organic products are available and always preferable.

Carob: Naturally sweet with a flavor similar to cocoa, carob contains protein, calcium, phosphorous, and some B vitamins without the caffeine of chocolate. Carob is sweet enough that it is unnecessary to add sugar to it, whereas cocoa is naturally bitter and a considerable amount of sugar is added to make it palatable.

Cayenne: Hot red chili pepper flakes (cayenne pepper) are a rich source of B vitamins, PABA, and vitamin C. The cayenne pepper's active oil is called capsicum. It is an energy and metabolism stimulant. It has been used medicinally to improve circulation and treat arthritis, ulcers, sore throats, and digestive disorders involving gas, nausea, or indigestion. It stimulates gastric secretions and peristaltic activity and soothes mucous linings.

Date Sugar: Date sugar is not as refined as cane sugar and contains many of the date's original vitamins and minerals such as folic acid. Ground dehydrated dates have a coarse granular texture and a mahogany color. Whole date puree is preferable to the dried sugar product because the puree contains the fiber that reduces its glycemic index. Purchase whole pitted dates and puree them in a blender with water to make a sweetener that can be added to cookies and other baked goods. Dates contain considerable amounts of soluble and insoluble fiber. Always purchase unsulfured, organically grown dates.

Dulse (Duhlss): Dulse is coarse-textured, red seaweed with a pungent, briny flavor. It grows around the British Isles and has a rubbery texture even when dried. Some Irish use it like a chewing tobacco. It is primarily used as flavoring in soups and as a condiment on salads and grains. It is available dried, granulated, powdered, or in sheets. Dulse is nutritionally rich in minerals, magnesium, fiber, vitamin C, beta-carotene, potassium, calcium, iron, and iodine. It is also high in trace minerals and is used as a treatment for thyroid disorders.

Edamame: Edamame is a simple dish made from young green soybeans and a bit of salt. The soybeans are picked when they are still sweet and green. They are great for a snack or as a green vegetable.

Essential Fatty Acids: Essential fatty acids (EFAs) are necessary for brain activity, immune system function, proper skin development, glandular function, and for all of the body's vital organs. They protect the cells from bacteria and viruses and are precursors to hormone production. They are essential, and Americans do not get enough of these healthful fats. There are EFAs in soy foods, nuts, seeds, and flaxseed oil.

Flaxseed: Flaxseed and flax oil contain lignans, which are natural chemicals that inhibit tumor progression and help balance estrogen as needed by the body. Flax also contains soluble and insoluble fiber and essential fatty acids. Raw flaxseed powder, flaxseed oil, and whole flaxseeds are all widely available. Buy whole flaxseeds, store them in the refrigerator, and grind into powder with a coffee grinder or food processor when ready to use.

All flaxseed products should have a fresh, nutty flavor. If the product starts to smell rancid or fishy, throw it out. Refrigerate all flaxseed products, as they are rich in natural oils that will become rancid if not protected. Flaxseed powder can also be used as an egg replacement.

If you have purchased more than you can use before it goes bad, use it in baking to add fiber without adding cholesterol. One tablespoon of flax powder and 3 tablespoons water equals 1 egg; mix and let stand for 30 seconds.

Definitions found on flaxseed product packaging:

Lignans—Associated more with the protein fraction of the fiber than with the oil component, lignans help the body regulate hormone levels, and protect against cancer.

Whole—The term whole means the seeds have not been processed. It is preferable to buy whole seeds, as the oils inside the tough outer coating have not been exposed to light and oxygen.

Powder—Prepowdered flaxseed can be purchased, but the oils have been released and will become rancid quickly. Be sure it is fresh. Check the pull date of the product and avoid if the pull date is within the time you would actually finish the product. It should smell sweet, nutty, and fresh. If it smells like the children's clay Play-Doh then it may be going bad.

Garlic: Garlic (*Allium sativum*) contains sulfur compounds, which have antimicrobial effects. Raw garlic and aged garlic are effective against staph, strep, bacillus, E. coli, salmonella, candida, roundworm, hookworm, and influenza. Garlic has potent cardiovascular benefits. Both raw and cooked garlic have been found to decrease triglyceride and cholesterol levels (total LDL), raise HDL cholesterol, lower blood pressure, and prevent excessive blood-clot formation. Raw garlic contains all of the potent medicinal properties, but the medicinal compounds break down and become less potent when cooked.

Genetically Altered Foods: Many packaged food products and whole foods are now genetically altered. They contain foreign DNA from insects, fish, bacteria, viruses, and even humans. Foods altered through genetic engineering often contain proteins and other components that have never before been part of the human diet. There is no way to predict whether those foods are safe to eat because they have not been rigorously tested before being released into our food supply.

There is considerable evidence that these foods are not safe to eat, may cause allergic reaction, may lead to the development of autoimmune disease, and have dramatically reduced nutritional and medicinal value. For example, natural organic soy foods contain powerful healthy phytochemicals, which fight cancer, osteoporosis, and menopausal symptoms. But the genetically altered soybeans are shadows of the real food and contain none of these nutrients.

Because these foods are not labeled as such at this time, the only way to avoid these foods is to buy foods labeled organic. Genetically altered foods are not allowed to be labeled organic. Buy organic whenever possible, particularly soy foods, corn and corn products, and dairy products.

Ginger: Gingerroot is useful in treating nausea, morning sickness, and motion sickness and has been used as a digestive and circulatory stimulant for thousands of years. Ginger can be purchased dried and ground in spice jars or in bulk or fresh in root form. The fresh root is recommended for cooking as it has superior flavor.

Glycemic Index: The glycemic index was devised to explain the apparent differences in the blood glucose response to similar amounts of carbohydrate. The standard for the glycemic index is a slice of white bread, which is assigned a value of 100. Each food has its own effects on blood sugar; some raise blood sugar more than others. For example, sweet potatoes have an index of 40 to 49 percent, while instant mashed potatoes have a more rapid response with a value of 80 to 90 percent. Soybeans are very low with a value of 10 to 19 percent, which makes them ideal for blood-sugar regulation.

Green Tea: Green tea contains numerous natural plant chemicals linked to the prevention and treatment of cancer and blood-sugar disorders. Catechins, for example, are linked to reduced rates of gastrointestinal cancers and are found in both green tea and black tea. Green tea is widely available in a caffeine-free form, as an extract, and as a dried leaf tea.

Guar Gum: Guar gum is a thickener obtained from the legume family of plants.

Hijiki (hee-JEE-kee): Hijiki, a dried black seaweed, has a slight anise flavor and nutty aroma. Usually dried into thin strips, it is available in both dried and fresh varieties at Asian markets, health-food stores, and mail-order companies. All sea vegetables have beneficial fiber that helps balance blood-sugar levels. Hijiki has a high mineral content and ten times more calcium by volume than milk, cheese, or other dairy products. It is also high in iron, protein, beta-carotene, B_1, potassium, and magnesium.

Honey: Honey contains fructose and glucose, enzymes, and nominal amounts of vitamins and some trace minerals. Honey is less processed than white sugar, which is made from cane and processed with chemicals to clean and bleach it. It is collected from flower nectar by bees and is actually sweeter than white sugar, and therefore it is possible to use less. Children under the age of two should never eat honey as it can transmit enough botulism to be very dangerous to them. Honey also can adversely effect blood-sugar levels, so it must be used sparingly and with a meal rather than on its own.

Irish Moss (Carrageenen [KEHR-ah-geen-an]): Irish moss fronds grow along the coast of Ireland and along North America's Atlantic coast. Its stubby, broad, forked fans grow in colors from reddish-purple to reddish-green. An extraction is used as a thickening agent and a food supplement because it contains calcium chloride. When used in cooking, the results are a bit softer than agar, but it can be used instead of agar in any recipe. Irish moss has the added benefit of containing iron, beta-carotene, and iodine.

Kelp: Kelp contains an easily assimilated form of minerals such as iron, potassium, calcium, iodine, and other trace minerals and vitamins. This is particularly beneficial for those with mineral deficiencies that have developed from a long-term fast-food diet. It can be purchased dried, granulated, or powdered.

Kombu (KOHM-boo): Kombu is part of the *Laminaria* family of sea vegetables and grows in long, dark-brown to grayish-black fronds up to 15 feet in length. It is harvested, sun-dried, and then folded into sheets. It is commonly used to make a flavorful broth or is added to bean recipes to increase their digestibility. It can be purchased dried in packages and stored indefinitely unopened. After opening, store in a cool dry place for up to six months. Kombu is a rich source of beta-carotene, vitamin B_2, vitamin C, calcium, and iodine.

Maple Syrup: True maple syrup comes from the sap of maple trees and is rich in potassium and calcium. It has a dark brown color and rich maple flavor. Many products claim to be maple syrup but upon closer inspection of the label, they are often made from cane sugar or corn syrup. True maple syrup has a superior flavor and is of higher nutritional value. There are also maple syrups flavored with synthetic sweeteners, which taste synthetic and carry the health risks of those synthetic sweeteners. Buy pure U.S. organic syrup for the highest quality, best flavor, and most nutritional value.

Miso: Miso, a smooth fragrant paste, is made from fermenting a mixture of whole soybeans and a grain such as rice or barley and is inoculated with *Aspergillus orzyae* bacteria. Miso is aged in cedar vats for one to three years.

Miso dissolves easily in water and is used to make soups and broth and to add flavoring to a wide variety of foods. Miso's medicinal properties include digestive enzymes and anticancer phytochemicals. Many flavors and varieties are available. Look for low-sodium miso.

Nori (NOH-ree): Nori is 48 percent protein by dry weight and is a rich source of vitamins, calcium, iron, and trace minerals. It is the most easily digestible of the seaweeds. Paper-thin sheets range in color from dark green to dark purple to black. It has a sweet subtle ocean flavor and is generally used for wrapping sushi, making rice balls, or for flavoring for soups and grains in Japan. It can be purchased toasted (labeled "yakinori"). Nori is also a rich source of fiber and bioavailable nutrients such as beta-carotene, thiamin (vitamin B_1), and niacin (vitamin B_3).

Nutritional Yeast: Nutritional yeast is a rich source of amino acids, calcium, potassium, phosphorus, magnesium, sodium, copper, iron, zinc, and B vitamins. Its cheesy flavor makes it a delicious topping for popcorn, sandwiches, tortillas, and soups.

Pears: Pears contain plant estrogens, along with the antioxidant and anti-carcinogen glutathione, and are recommended for the prevention of high blood pressure, stroke, and menopausal symptoms. They contain potassium, pectins, hemicellulose, vitamin C, folic acid, potassium, manganese, and selenium. Hemicellulose is an indigestible complex carbohydrate or fiber source in pears, which promotes the beneficial intestinal flora necessary for digestion and elimination in the colon.

Pumpkin: Pumpkin is rich in beta-carotene and has been purported to have benefit for prostate disorders, stomach problems, worms, and morning sickness.

Raspberries: These dark berries are low on the glycemic index and contain natural phytochemicals that help prevent conditions such as infections, heart disease, and stroke. They also contain vitamin C, calcium, magnesium, and iron.

Recombinant Bovine Growth Hormone (rBGH):
Recombinant bovine growth hormone is a genetically altered product injected into cows to make them produce more milk. Traces of rBGH are found in much of the milk in stores today. Because it is a new chemical in our food supply, there are questions about its safety. There is some evidence that ingestion of rBGH disrupts hormone development in humans and is particularly dangerous for children. Therefore, buy only organic milk and dairy products to avoid all rBGH-tainted products.

Roasted Soy Nuts: Soy nuts are made from whole soybeans that have been soaked and then roasted. Similar in taste to peanuts (another legume), these are available in a variety of flavors and are perfect for snacks. Look for those seasoned without salt or make them at home.

Sea Salt: Sea salt is a mineral-rich, unprocessed salt that contains magnesium, manganese, boron, copper, silicon, iron, sodium chloride, and nickel. It is superior in flavor and nutritional value to table salt and is available through health-food stores and many grocery stores.

Sea Vegetables: Sea vegetables contain alginate fiber, which reduces the gastric emptying rate in humans and helps to regulate blood sugar. Sea vegetables also contain minerals such as iodine (necessary for proper thyroid function) and omega-3 fatty acids and are an excellent dietary fiber source for preventing or treating fiber-deficient related diseases. They are a rich source of calcium, iron, magnesium, carotenoids, vitamin C, vitamin E, and the B vitamins (including B_{12}), amino acids, bromine, and phosphorus. Sea vegetables are available through natural food markets and through the mail-order companies listed in the back of this book. *See also* dulse, hijiki, Irish moss, kelp, kombu, nori, and wakame.

Soy: Whole black or yellow soybeans are available dried or canned, and young green soybeans (edamame) are available fresh in Asian markets and frozen in many grocery and health-food stores. Soybeans are also used to make foods such as soy milk, miso, tempeh, textured vegetable protein (TVP), and soy protein powders. Soy foods contain calcium, essential fatty acids, protein, and iron. The whole beans are a rich source of soluble and insoluble fiber, and all soy foods are cholesterol free.

Organic soybeans, those that are not genetically altered, also contain various substances, that fight cancer, help stabilize hormones, prevent osteoporosis, and help maintain blood-sugar levels. Soy foods help prevent and treat heart disease, by helping to reduce LDL cholesterol, and they have a favorable effect on blood pressure and weight management.

Soy Cheese and Soy Yogurt: Soy cheese and yogurt are made from soy milk. These products contain no cholesterol and no lactose, whey, or casein. They are available in a variety of flavors, but they taste very different from dairy cheese or yogurt. Some soy cheeses melt well; others do not. The cheeses with flavor added such as smoky cheddar or jalapeño, tend to be more popular. The yogurts often have a strong fruit or citrus flavor, which lends itself well to fruit compote rather than eating the yogurt alone.

Soy Milk: Soy milk is made from boiling ground whole soybeans in water and separating the liquid from the fiber. Soy milk provides an alternative for those with dairy allergies or lactose intolerance. Lactose is the milk sugar that 30 to 50 million Americans have a hard time digesting. Soy milk can also be used to replace milk for those choosing a vegetarian diet.

Organic soy milk is made from soybeans grown without chemicals and offers an alternative to cow's milk, which could very well be tainted with hormones, such as rBGH and antibiotics, which are commonly used in dairy farming at this time. Some people choose soy for its benefits, such as the blood-sugar-regulating effects of its fiber or the menopausal regulating effects of the phytochemicals.

Soy milks are available in plain, cocoa, carob, vanilla, cinnamon, and almond flavors. Some are sweetened and some are not. Some are fortified, meaning they have supplements added to them, just like dairy milk. Calcium and vitamin D are now added to some soy milks. Soy milk has a higher protein content than the rice milk alternatives. Fat content varies just as with dairy milks, and nonfat, low-fat, and whole varieties are available.

Soy Protein Powder: Instant soy protein powder quickly mixes into any liquid. It can be blended with fruit juice and a banana to make a smoothie.

Soy Sprouts: Soy sprouts are similar to mung bean sprouts. They are a good source of calcium.

Stevia (STEH-via): Stevia is a safe, natural alternative to refined sugar and artificial sweeteners. The Native Americans of Paraguay have used this herb for centuries. Stevia is now available through health-food stores in the United States. The extract from the leaves of this herb can be up to six hundred times sweeter than sugar; therefore, just a tiny amount is all that is necessary.

It is one of the few sweeteners available that does not appear to raise blood-sugar levels. It contains no calories and is an ideal sweetener for people with diabetes or hypoglycemia. It is available in liquid or powdered form. See mail-order sources listed in the back of book. Products vary in flavor and strength and should be used according to the manufacturer's recommendations.

Strawberries: Strawberries are a rich source of vitamin C and contain potassium, manganese, and biotin. They are also a good source of phytochemicals such as phytoesterols and polyphenols (compounds that may have antiviral activity), and glutathione, a powerful antioxidant and anticarcinogen.

Tofu: Curdling fresh hot soy milk, in a process similar to making cottage cheese, results in tofu curds. The resulting curds are pressed together giving the product the consistency of soft cheese. Tofu is available in various textures including extra firm, firm, medium, soft, and silken. When using tofu, keep in mind that tofu provides the texture and the nutrition, it's up to you to provide the flavor. Firm and extra firm tofu is best used for stir-fry, grilling, baking, or any time you need the tofu to hold its shape. Medium soft tofu is a good choice for puddings, fillings, cheesecakes, and salads. Silken and soft can be used to make creamy desserts, frostings, and savory dressings and dips or for recipes that call for blending tofu.

Tempeh (TEM-pay): Tempeh is mashed soybeans, lightly cooked, inoculated with *Rhizopus oligosporus* bacteria, and formed into inch-thick slabs. Specialty tempeh are made by mixing soybeans with rice, millet, or other grains. The result is a tender cake with a smoky or nutty taste and an aroma reminiscent of mushrooms. It is a good substitute for meat in stews, chilies, casseroles, and soups.

Turbinado Sugar: Turbinado sugar is cane sugar that has not been bleached or highly processed. It contains much if its original vitamins and minerals and does not contain the processing chemicals of bleached white table sugar.

Tvp: Texturized vegetable protein is a product obtained from soybeans in a process where the ground beans are spun and extruded to create an almost pure protein. Tvp makes an excellent meat substitute because of its protein content and its meatlike consistency. Tvp is often sold as a bulk item in natural foods stores. There are also several products that will include TVP as an ingredient in taco and sloppy joe mixes.

Vanilla Extract: Also known as vanillan and ethyl vanillan, vanilla can be used in small quantities to add a sweet flavor to recipes and drinks. Mexican extracts are even stronger than domestic products and require just a drop to flavor a smoothie, for example.

Wakame (wah-KAH-meh): This olive-colored kelp grows in winglike fronds. The dark brown variety is more strongly flavored. Wakame is high in calcium, iron, beta-carotene, niacin, and protein. It is available through Asian markets, health-food stores, and mail-order companies.

Whole Soybeans: Soybeans mature in the pod into a hard dry bean. Whole soybeans can be used in soups and stews as other dried beans.

Yogurt: Yogurt is naturally rich in the healthful bacteria needed in our intestines for proper digestion and absorption of nutrients. It is also high in calcium and magnesium. Those who cannot digest other dairy products generally can tolerate yogurt. Fresh, plain, nonfat unsweetened yogurt is best because it can be purchased free of sugar and additives.

Mail-Order Companies

Bob's Red Mill—Natural Foods, Inc.
5209 SE International Way
Milwaukee, OR 97222
Phone: (503) 654-3215
Fax: (503) 653-1339
Call or fax for a free catalog. This company carries bean flours, barley products, whole grain hot cereals, corn products, dried fruits, flaxseed, kasha, and rice products.

Cheryl's Herbs
836 Hanley Industrial Court
St. Louis, MO 63144
Phone: (800) 231-5971
Fax: (314) 963-4454
E-mail: pawgep@aol.com
Website: www.cherylsherbs.com
Call the toll-free number and request a free catalog. This company has a line of stevia products including stevia leaf powder and stevia extract powder.

Herbal Advantage, Inc.
131 Bobwhite Road
Rogerville, MO 65742-9214
Phone: (800) 753-9199
Fax: (417) 753-2000

Website: www.herbaladvantage.com
Call the toll-free number for a free catalog or stevia recipe book.

Mountain Ark Trading Company
Macrobiotic Company of America (MCOA)—
Wholesale Division
799 Old Leicester Highway
Asheville, NC 28806
Phone: (800) 438-4730
Call the toll-free number for a free catalog. This company is the leading supplier of traditional and organic products in the United States and carries such products as organic grains, miso, seaweeds, barley malt syrup, black beans, and sesame oils.

Omega Nutrition
6515 Aldrich Road
Bellingham, WA 98226
Phone: (800) 661-FLAX (3529)
Fax: (604) 253-4228
This company carries the sweetener stevia, kefir, and whole flax and flax oil. Call the toll-free number to order a catalog.

Uwajimaya
516 Sixth Avenue South
Seattle, WA 98104
Phone: (800) 889-1928
Call the toll-free number for a free catalog. This Asian market carries an extensive array of macrobiotic products: soy foods including the young green soybeans for edamame; green tea; bamboo steamers; and sea vegetables such as arame, hijiki, kombu, nori, and kelp.

Walnut Acres Organic Farms
Walnut Acres Road
Penns Creek, PA 17862
Phone: (800) 433-3998
Website: www.walnutacres.com
Call for a free catalog. Walnut Acres Organic Farms offers a complete line of natural products and kitchen tools including unrefined/unbleached sugars, juices, organic fruits and vegetables, canned soups, and cookies.

Wisdom of the Ancients
640 South Perry Lane
Tempe, AZ 85281
Phone: (800) 899-9908
Websites: www.wisdomherbs.com and www.steviaplus.com
Call for a list of the company's stevia products.

Index